THE MOBIUS MODEL

A Guide for Developing Effective Relationships in Groups, Teams, and Organizations

by
Larry Demarest, Ph.D.
Marjorie Herdes
Joyce Stockton, Ph.D.
Will Stockton, Ph.D.

Out beyond ideas of wrongdoing and rightdoing,
there is a field. I'll meet you there.
—Rumi

MMI Group, LLC

Copyright 2004 by The MMI Group, LLC

Published for The MMI Group, LLC by
Farrar & Associates

ISBN 0-9719978-2-9

Library of Congress Cataloging-in-Publication Data
A catalog record for this book is available from the Library of Congress

Interior design by Rachel Holscher
Cover design by David Spohn
Composition by Stanton Publication Services, Inc., St. Paul, MN

For additional copies of this book, contact

The MMI Group, LLC
4255 Meadowbrook Blvd.
Minneapolis, MN 55416

Myers-Briggs Type Indicator® and MBTI® are registered trademarks of the Myers-Briggs Type Indicator Trust in the United States and other countries.

Table of Contents

❧ ❧ ❧ ❧ ❧

Preface

❧ ❧ ❧ ❧ ❧

When I was still relatively new to the business world and working for Honeywell as a quality improvement facilitator, I attended a weeklong training session that focused on the latest approaches to quality. I returned from it eager to share with the engineers and managers what seemed to me to be outstanding tools for improving our processes for design and production. I was stunned that my colleagues responded with indifference and resistance to the proposed tools and techniques. I quickly realized that I had no idea how to facilitate their commitment to develop new capabilities.

About this same time, I heard about an organization development group that was using a unique model to guide their communication that resulted in clear, shared commitments and action. The group had a reputation for testing their assumptions and approaches on themselves before recommending them to any client. I thought it was worth investigating.

I learned that William Stockton, a cultural anthropologist and member of the group, had developed the Mobius Model as a way to explicate his philosophical assumptions and test them in his life and work. The Mobius Model is a practical guide, formulated from a simple set of principles, for acting in ways that honor the contribution that each individual brings to our shared experience. The model has been used and tested in practice as a guide for development and collaboration, nationally and internationally, since 1979.

I found the model unique in the way it made complicated human interaction and development seem clear and logical. I left Honeywell and went into partnership with William in Mobius, Inc., an organization development practice. Over the last fourteen years, I have seen from experience that, with the Mobius Model as a guide, it is possible to create work environments in which people commit to learn together how to flourish and be productive.

The work that William and I enjoy the most is facilitating dialogues involving hundreds of people with strong differences on very controversial issues, i.e., union management or community-wide education issues. We don't always explain the model, although we always use it to guide our work. When we do share the model explicitly with people who are reluctant to participate in learning about "communications issues"—those who say things like, "Oh no, we aren't going to go into that swamp, are we?"—they respond that the model relieves their sense of frustration and confusion. I also found that using the model as a guide in my personal life over the years immeasurably eased my life as a single parent of two teenagers.

I once took a course in rock climbing. I was prepared to be scared and inept, and I knew that I had a lot to learn. In this situation, I was willing to be lost and confused. In my work life, I find it more difficult to acknowledge that I am lost. I am less likely to recognize and welcome my confusion. But I have learned, with the Mobius Model as a guide, that I can't be any help to others or myself unless I'm willing to be a learner in every moment. I need to recognize when I am lost and be open to learning from others.

This is the challenge we put to you, the reader: Be willing to be lost, to acknowledge that you don't know when you don't, to approach relationships as an unfolding adventure, and to listen to learn. In our society, where we are encouraged from birth to be smart and right, it is difficult to acknowledge that we don't have the answers—that our viewpoint is limited. The only way that new possibilities can come into view is if you and I hold our points of view lightly, with a willingness to see in new ways. The leaders and facilitators that are able to lead most creatively and productively are those who are willing to listen to learn. This is the challenge: Explore your own points of view to see if you can recognize areas where you are not open to new ideas. The Mobius Model serves as a road map for that exploration if you are willing to see that you are lost and if you then pay careful attention to the map. We have laid out the map in detail.

This introduction to the Mobius Model is designed to familiarize you with practical applications and tools you can put to use.

- Chapter 1 is an introduction to the adventure of relationship development; it defines and illustrates the key ideas underlying the Mobius Model.
- Chapter 2 provides a guide for recognizing when you are "lost" and for taking the critical first step to turn potentially troublesome conversations into creative ones.
- Chapter 3 illustrates in detail the qualities that mark important turns in the path of relationship development and provides ways to circle back when you get lost.
- Chapter 4 illustrates how the Mobius Model is a guide for working with individuals, groups, organizations, and communities.
- The conclusion points to additional steps you can take, should you choose to continue to develop your skills.

The book was written in a four-way partnership (The MMI Group, LLC)—by William Stockton; Joyce Stockton, a family therapist and Will's wife of forty-one years; Larry Demarest, an educator, trainer, and longtime friend and colleague; and me, Marjorie Herdes, Will's partner in Mobius, Inc. Writing it was a collaborative effort that has been a satisfying and developmental challenge for us all—a true expression of the Mobius process. We hope this book will contribute to dialogues about how to develop collaborative and productive relationships in all aspects of life.

꙳ ꙳ ꙳ ꙳ ꙳

CHAPTER ONE

The Mobius Model

How much of what you do each day is accomplished by talking and interacting with others? Consider your interactions broadly—the one-to-one conversations, the meetings that you attend as leader or participant, the interactions with your work group or other groups.

Can you put a percentage on it—15, 45, 75 percent or higher? When we ask this question in workshops, most people's responses seem to fall between 80 and 85 percent, with some even answering 100 percent. It is rare that anyone says that less than half of what they get done results from conversations.

Even if half—and surely if most—of your effectiveness is tied to your ability to have successful interactions with others, then you'd probably benefit from a road map that would guide you toward positive and creative interactions and away from unproductive ones. *The Mobius Model* can provide you with just such a guide and equip you to use it in your daily interactions.

In his more than twenty-five years of actively researching interactions, William Stockton discovered that conversations that create satisfying results have identifiable components, which flow in a particular sequence. *The Mobius Model*, authored by Stockton, depicts these components and the sequence in which they unfold. It serves as a guide for positively affecting the interactions we all depend on to get things done.

During interactions, those who are participants in a conversation as well as those who guide groups

(e.g., leaders, facilitators, coaches, or team builders) can use the model.

CONVERSATIONS FOR RELATIONSHIP DEVELOPMENT

At its core, the Mobius Model is about the development of human relationships—couples, friendships, families, groups and teams, organizations, communities, and nations—and the conversations that facilitate this development. The Mobius Model focuses on the kinds of conversations people have because conversations are the main vehicle for developing relationships or for impeding their development.

What Do We Mean by *Development*?

Many factors influence the ways we change over the course of our lives. Sometimes the influence is formal learning—we are taught to make calculations in arithmetic. Sometimes it is informal learning—we learn to use a computer program by trying it out. Physical growth is a factor—we become taller and heavier. Occasionally, luck or random success leads to change—something we try works, so we keep on doing it. Many other factors are also involved.

Development is a part of human growth and change, but *development is distinguished by a qualitative change in capacity.* Consider a caterpillar turning into a butterfly. At first the caterpillar changes quantitatively as it grows bigger—just more caterpillar. Then at some point, it becomes a butterfly. Its transformation into a butterfly is an obvious qualitative change. We see that a butterfly has new capacities that the caterpillar lacks. It can fly.

We recognize and often enjoy observing individual development, taking special note when very young children gain the ability to talk and to walk. Older children learn to use computers, play musical instruments, and participate in sports. We are aware that development continues over the lifespan as children "grow up," complete education programs, take jobs, and often marry and become parents. As adults, we continue to develop, even though the qualitative changes that mark our development may be less obvious.

What Do We Mean by *Relationship Development?*

The focus of the Mobius Model is on the development of relationships, not individuals. This book focuses primarily on the development of groups and teams. While most people are aware of individual development, the development of relationships is less widely acknowledged and understood. For many people, groups just are—some are productive and some are not, some are enjoyable and some are not. A common attitude about groups is that they are what they are, and no one individual can do much about them. We often do not recognize that it is possible for groups and teams, other than sports teams, to develop and increase their capacity to function effectively.

Of course, these two kinds of development— the development of individuals and the development of relationships—are related to one another. The Mobius Model assumes that relationships can develop only if the individuals in those relationships are willing and able to develop.

At the same time, it is in the context of a particular relationship that individual development comes into play. Individuals may develop capacities that they use in some relationships but not in others. Robert, for example, may be skillful in working through conflicts with his wife, but he avoids conflict at the office. If Robert and his teammates became capable of handling their conflicts, that new capability would be an example of relationship development.

> ### Barb and Laura: An Example
>
> Let's say that two colleagues, Barb and Laura, have been asked to carry out a project to plan an upcoming conference. Barb wants to make a detailed plan before beginning. She argues that such a plan will make it more likely that the project will succeed, and it will help prepare them for any surprises along the way. This approach has worked well for her in the past.
>
> Laura does not want to take time to create a detailed plan. She prefers a general plan in which more detail is added as the project evolves. To her, there are so many unknowns in this project that it would not be a good use of time to try to anticipate all the possible twists and turns. She is confident that they can shape a good plan as they deal with the actualities of the project.
>
> Each person feels strongly about her approach and is convinced that it is the best route to success. Their discussions so far have been unsuccessful. Privately, each of them is considering requesting that their supervisor name a new partner or remove them from the project.

Seemingly, Laura and Barb do not have the skills and perspectives needed to work through this situation. Even if they are able to do this in other relationships, they apparently can't or don't want to in this one.

An opportunity for developing the capacity of their relationship has presented itself. From the point of view of relationship development, this is an important choice point. Barb and Laura can (1) request to be removed from this project or (2) ask to work with a different, more compatible partner. If they make either of these choices, they will also be choosing not to develop their relationship *at this time*. They can also (3) choose to work on this issue together and hence develop their relationship. What would that mean, and how would they do it?

Developing a relationship means discovering new ways to think, communicate, and interact *together*. For Barb and Laura, that would mean figuring out a way to work with their different approaches to planning so that both approaches are honored, and a "solution" that works for both of them is discovered.

More importantly, if they can develop a way to get "unstuck" this time, they can use it the next time they have different approaches or opinions that seem at odds with one another. This is what it means to develop a relationship: They will now have ways of understanding and interacting that they didn't have before, and they will have increased their capacity to have a more productive and satisfying relationship.

How could they do this? The Mobius Model provides a road map for working through this kind of situation so that new capacities are developed and the participants are more satisfied. Barb and Laura have already acknowledged that they have different methods of beginning a project and that these differences are getting in the way of moving ahead together in a timely fashion. If they can further acknowledge that, while each person's way is important to that individual, it is not the only way or the "right" way, they can also make a choice to develop their relationship.

Chapter 2 illustrates how Barb and Laura can use the Mobius Model to develop their relationship in such a way that they will get the job done *and* gain a qualitatively different way to work together. Depending on their own levels of skill and comfort, they may be able to work through this process on their own, or they may choose to engage a coach or facilitator to assist them. The first step, however, is making a mutual choice to develop their relationship.

FEATURES OF THE MOBIUS MODEL

Before going on to illustrate how the Mobius Model serves as a guide to productive interactions, there are five key characteristics of the model that we want to highlight:

The Mobius Model guides creative conversations, interactions where something that the participants want—such as a shared vision, a new product, an improved sense of morale and teamwork,

or increased collaboration—is created. Using the Mobius Model as a guide, satisfying and productive interactions can become the rule rather than the exception—a matter of choice, not chance.

The Mobius Model brings into view our inner and outer conversations. The image and metaphor for the Mobius Model comes from the Mobius strip, illuminated by the nineteenth-century German mathematician August Mobius.

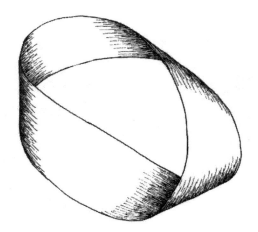

The unique feature of this strip is that it has only one surface. If you were to run your finger along it, your finger would travel from what appears to be the outside of the strip to what appears to be the inside and back to the outside without leaving the surface—the Mobius strip is one surface that seemingly flows from inside to outside.

The Mobius strip is used as the metaphor for these intentional conversations to remind us that there are always two aspects of every conversation—an outer conversation and an inner one. When one person is speaking out loud (the outer conversation), those listening are nearly always engaged in a simultaneous inner conversation. Inner conversations might be about what the speaker has said (e.g., "What a great opportunity," "I wonder how long this is going to last?" or "If the company really makes that change, I could lose my job"), or they might be about something totally unrelated ("Tomorrow I really have to finish that proposal," or "Let's hope that our dental insurance covers Phil's braces").

The person who is speaking the outer conversation can also have an inner conversation going on at the same time. For example, a speaker addressing a group might be saying to her- or himself, "This is going well; I think they like it," or "They don't seem very interested; I suppose they've heard all this before."

As an example, let's say your boss asks you to take on a new project, and your outer conversation, the one both you and your boss can hear, is, "Sure, I'd be glad to do that." But what is your inner conversation, the one only you can hear? It might be congruent with your outer talk: "This is great; I'm finally getting a chance to show what I know." Or it might diverge from the outer: "I can't believe this. Doesn't the boss know how much I'm doing right now? I can't possibly take on another project, get it all done, and stay sane!"

Generally speaking, relationships and interactions go better—are healthier and more satisfying and productive—if our inner and outer conversations are aligned. When the inner and outer conversations aren't consistent, we may find ourselves self-editing and end up feeling like we really can't bring what we have to contribute to this relationship or interaction. When these two conversations diverge on a regular basis, we become cynical or angry (perhaps we raise our voice), or we become discouraged, feeling that it is not safe to reveal our thoughts or feelings. In either case, our relationship with that person or group will probably fail to produce satisfying results.

The Mobius Model reminds us that every conversation contains at least two different, but connected, perspectives. The cartoon below captures this quality. While these two fellows seem to believe that they are on opposite sides, following the strip around will allow them to see that they are on the same side; it's only an illusion that they appear to be in opposition to one another.

Acknowledging that apparently conflicting viewpoints are in fact complementary, and that each contains part of the "truth," is problematic for many people, particularly when one point of view is seen as "right" and the other "wrong." However, relationship development hinges on being able to see the common ground that emerges when opposing views are fully explored, truly understood, and brought together to form a more complete representation. Any single point of view is limited and cannot reveal the depth that additional viewpoints provide.

DON'T SHOOT!

WE MAY BOTH BE ON THE SAME SIDE.

AshleighBrilliant.com

The Mobius Model calls on us to focus on the present moment during our interactions. It is often easy to dwell on the past, particularly when an unsatisfying past seems to have been someone else's fault. It is also tempting to drift toward worrying about what might happen in the future, to wonder if you are up to the challenge ahead. Of course, healthy adults are aware of and learn from the past, but they don't stay stuck there. They look forward to the future and use today to prepare for it, but they don't live in the future, either.

> "In order to be utterly happy the only thing necessary is to refrain from comparing this moment with other moments in the past, which I often did not fully enjoy because I was comparing them with other moments of the future."—Andre Gide

The present conversation, the interaction we are having now—not the one we had last week or last month or last year, and not the one we wish we would have tomorrow or next week or the next time we are with this person or group—is the only place where we can create something different. Only *now* can we take action to alter the habits and patterns that keep our interactions stuck.

The Mobius Model provides a way to use the energy in our judgments about ourselves and others to begin a creative conversation. Noncreative conversations are often characterized by blame or worry and repeat the patterns that keep us stuck. These judgments call attention to potentially powerful sources of creativity that can be used to bring about new patterns of interaction, if we choose.

THE MOBIUS QUALITIES

Six essential qualities of relationships were identified during the research and development of the Mobius Model. These are briefly defined below and described more fully in chapter 3.

- **Mutual Understanding** exists when each person feels understood and also understands the other(s). It is important to note that mutual understanding is not the same as agreement. We can understand others without necessarily agreeing with them.
- **Possibility** exists when everyone recognizes something new that is desirable and seems realistic to create.
- **Commitment** exists when there is agreement to priorities among the goals and values that will direct action.
- **Capability** exists when there is agreement to a way to fulfill the commitments to which everyone has agreed.
- **Responsibility** exists when there is agreement to expectations about what each person or unit will do to carry out the commitments.
- **Acknowledgment** exists when there is mutual recognition of what has been accomplished and what is still missing for the commitments to be fully realized.

Though they may seem abstract, these qualities are real and can be recognized as present or absent in a particular relationship or interaction. It can be challenging to capture their depth and complexity in words, so we refer to things we can observe or experience to let us know whether a quality is present or missing. The qualities can be recognized in three different ways—the language of everyday speech, the patterns of interaction we observe, and the feelings we experience in the relationship.

Take love, for example. Love is hard to define satisfactorily for many people, so we often look for indications that love exists in our words and actions: what is said and not said, what is done and not done. Yet even though we use such indicators of love, we wouldn't say that love itself is only what we do and say; we recognize that it is much larger and more complex than that.

The qualities of the Mobius Model are similar. For example, in its fullest expression, Mutual Understanding is a confidence that we are understood and understand others, an awareness that we can be ourselves in a relationship, and the recognition that we are all part of the same whole. As such, Mutual Understanding is hard to describe fully, so to see if it is present, we look for indicators such as people saying they feel understood, feeling free to speak their minds, and giving energy to listening to and understanding others.

Experiencing the Qualities: An Example

Imagine that you are a new employee in an organization and are attending your first meeting of the work team to which you have been assigned. You arrive at the meeting a few minutes early and introduce yourself to Sylvia, the only other person in the room. You mention that you are new to the organization and that this is your first team meeting.

In response, Sylvia says to you: "Well, I hope someone clued you in about this team. We've been stuck in the same place for a long time. If you ask me, it will never get any better around here."

Sylvia's statement conveys the absence of the Mobius quality called Possibility. One indicator that Possibility is present is the belief that problematic situations can be improved. Sylvia's speech conveys that she does not believe this is possible for this team. Sylvia alone may have this perspective, or it may also be shared and reinforced by other team members and be a definite influence on the team's culture.

Several months later, there is a reorganization, and you are assigned to another team that will be meeting in three days. Matt, the team leader, calls and asks if he can stop by to talk with you sometime before the meeting. When you two meet, he orients you to the work of the team and briefly tells you a little bit about the other members. He is careful to familiarize you with the team's ground rules about how they want to work together and the values they strive to adhere to. He also goes over the particular goals the team is working on for the next three months.

Spelling out and agreeing to particular goals and values is an indication that Commitment is present for this team. And, indeed, as you begin to work with this group, the goals and values are often referred to and actively used to allocate resources and assess the team's progress.

THE MOBIUS MODEL AS A ROAD MAP FOR CREATIVE INTERACTIONS

When traveling by car, road maps can be helpful in several ways. To begin with, a map shows you a way to reach your destination. In addition, it provides milestones that you can use to check your progress and see if you are on track in getting where you want to go. Finally, if you get lost or off track, you can trace your route backward to see where you got off course and how to get back on.

When seeking to develop relationships, the Mobius Model can be equally helpful as a relationship map. Like a highway road map,

- The Mobius Model *shows you a way* to your destination.
- The six qualities of the Mobius Model—Mutual Understanding, Possibility, Commitment, Capability, Responsibility, and Acknowledgment—serve as *milestones* to guide you on your way. They show the sequence and the signposts. For example, if you were driving from New York City to Washington, D.C., you would expect to pass through New Jersey, Delaware, and Maryland before reaching your destination. If you are on a Mobius journey and you have just left Mutual Understanding, then you can expect to pass through Possibility next, and then on to Commitment and the other Mobius milestones.
- When you are lost, the Mobius Model can help you get *back on track*. In many relationships, a typical response to something that is not working is to do more of what isn't working. Say that your team had recently agreed on the top three goals for the next three months. Later, you hear several members say they are not clear about the current priorities. So you call a meeting and go back through the process of clarifying the priorities. To your puzzlement, a few

days later, another member tells you she doesn't think those are the most important things to accomplish. What would you do next?

Rather than getting angry with the dissenting team member or returning once again to goal and priority setting, the Mobius Model suggests a different approach—look back over the way you came for a possible explanation of this situation. For commitment to be true and lasting, for example, the parties making the commitment need to believe that what they are committing to is possible and important. If it seems pie-in-the-sky or peripheral to them, they won't really be committed, and you will observe confusion, resistance, and go-along behavior rather than real dedication and consistent follow-through.

To trace your journey back another step, if Possibility doesn't seem feasible or important to some team members, then revisiting Mutual Understanding may be called for. People will not see as possible, and therefore will not commit to, goals and a course of action that is not based on understanding and taking into account everyone's viewpoint. Perhaps Mutual Understanding was missing, had not been achieved during the course of setting goals or priorities, and thus needs attention now. (Or perhaps it had been present,

but in the meantime something occurred requiring that it be revisited and created again.)

This is the counsel of the Mobius Model. When there is difficulty at one step, rather than redoubling efforts at that step, retrace your route to see if the trouble is being caused by something that happened or failed to happen during a prior stage.

SUMMARY

The Mobius Model identifies the qualities of satisfying and productive relationships and depicts the sequence in which they develop. Using the model as a guide, we can

- Identify which qualities are already present in a particular relationship
- Recognize those qualities that are not yet developed and hence missing
- Facilitate conversations to develop the missing qualities

The interactions involved in developing relationships frequently involve one of two underlying communication modes, monologue and dialogue. Before showing (in chapters 3 and 4) how the Mobius Model can serve as a guide for development, we will distinguish two very different kinds of conversations that must be understood in order to use the Mobius Model effectively as a road map.

❦ ❦ ❦ ❦ ❦

CHAPTER TWO

Monologue and Dialogue

Sometimes what you say leads to trouble. Have you ever found yourself deep into a conversation before you noticed that something has gone terribly wrong? Have you ever tried to help a situation with the best of intentions and found you made things worse? Do you sometimes know you have the right answer but no one will listen?

Sometimes what you don't say leads to trouble. Have you ever kept quiet when you thought something didn't seem right, and it turns out you were right? Have you ever let an opportunity pass you by because you didn't ask for the help you needed?

This chapter is about how to understand and respond creatively to these kinds of situations. You will learn to recognize the natural human reactions that get you and others into trouble. You will learn how to respond differently to these challenging moments with conversations that lead to development. We will return to Laura and Barb (who are trying to manage the conference together) to see how their relationship could take a creative turn.

The research behind the Mobius Model reveals that our interactions often involve conversations that take two characteristic forms—monologue or dialogue. These patterns of communication express the Mobius qualities differently, and they have very different effects on the development of relationships.

Conversations driven by *monologues* act to limit development by distracting our attention from the present moment and concentrating it on past events or future concerns. Monologues are stories based on judgments that someone is "wrong" and should change, or judgments that someone is "right" and others should change to be more like him or her.

"Let us not look back to the past with anger, nor towards the future with fear, but look around with awareness."
—James Thurber

In monologues, we express a point of view with an expectation that others will listen and learn; we ourselves do not expect to listen and learn.

These conversations occur every day, and you will probably recognize them. Sometimes in families, teams, or organizations the same stories are repeated so often that they become a habitual part of daily communication. Without question, monologues are the dominant reaction to differing viewpoints in our culture. Monologues tend to separate us from others, with some people included and others excluded, some being up and others down. We may seem to have a positive bond with those who agree with our monologues (e.g., you and I may base our interactions on our shared dislike of Sally); however, these kinds of bonds rarely lead to relationships that develop over time.

It may sound like we are saying that monologues are bad. Monologues are natural human reactions to differences, and our monologues call attention to what makes life vibrant and interesting.

Note that all the color in the Mobius Model graphic (see cover) is in the monologues. Without monologues, life would be vanilla pudding—no lumps, no bumps, no variety, no learning from each other. However, we must bring our monologues—our personal "truths"—into dialogue with others to reap the contributions that they can make. For example, if I am angry with a friend for being late, my monologue might go something like this: "You are always late! You need to get your life more organized so that you can keep the commitments you make!" When I am angry with her, it is because I think she is more capable than I see her being. If I tell my friend my monologue, it will not sound like an acknowledgment of her capability. I must bring my point of view (my monologue) into dialogue with her in a way that she can hear as respectful, and I will need to listen compassionately to understand how she experiences herself and her situation. This kind of dialogue can lead to learning for both of us and a deepening of our friendship.

Fear-based monologues can also make a contribution if I see that my fears point to a challenge and an opportunity to grow that I have not yet chosen. For example, if you ask me if I want to be a rocket pilot, I'll just laugh. I don't feel a bit of fear. However, if you ask me if I want to go hang gliding, the palms of my hands will start to sweat, and I do experience fear. I'm feeling fearful because hang gliding is something I might actually do if I don't let my fear stop me. If I am able to recognize that I have a monologue, a point of view that may not be the whole truth, then I have an opportunity to see myself another

way—to see that hang gliding is possible for me. Monologues are gifts to us if we bring them into dialogue and learn from them. If we believe our monologues are the whole truth, we don't learn, we stay stuck, and so do our relationships.

Our monologues can be shared in *dialogue* in ways that create partnership and collaboration with those with whom we differ. In dialogue there is a respectful sharing of differing viewpoints that leads to Mutual Understanding. Such understanding forms the basis for a shared vision, commitment to goals and values, and collaborative action.

Dialogue requires the willingness to listen to understand others who see situations differently than we do and to share our points of view honestly until each feels fully understood. Listening to understand means putting aside the temptation to agree, disagree, commiserate, or fix the situation and, instead, to listen respectfully in order to understand and to learn. When we feel strongly about our own position, listening for understanding can be very challenging.

MONOLOGUE AND DIALOGUE ON THE MOBIUS MODEL

These patterns of communication are shown on the Mobius Model (on page 11). The outer circles depict the flow and unfolding of the four monologue conversations. Blame and Praise monologues flow counterclockwise, and Worry and Claim monologues flow clockwise. The monologues are described as being "outside" the circle, where the focus is on the *qualities of individuals*, either self or others.

The process of dialogue is shown on the inside of the Mobius Model diagram, where the focus is on the *qualities of the relationship* between self and others.

The arrow at the top of the circle represents the choice we have when confronting differences. We can choose to engage in monologues that make our differences a source of misunderstanding and division, or we can choose to bring our differences into dialogue so that we

---

"In a true dialogue, both sides are willing to change. We have to appreciate that the truth can be received from outside of—not only within—our own group. If we do not believe that, entering into a dialogue would be a waste of time. If we think we monopolize the truth and we still organize a dialogue, it is not authentic. We have to believe that by engaging in dialogue with the other person, we have the possibility of making a change within ourselves, that we can become deeper."—Thich Nhat Hanh

The Mobius Model™
A Guide for Creative Dialogue

can understand each other and discover common ground for collaboration and relationship building.

The Monologues

> "Every man takes the limits of his field of vision for the limits of the world."—Arthur Schopenhauer

The Mobius Model distinguishes four monologues: Blame, Worry, Praise, and Claim. Blame and Worry monologues contain "negative" stories, and Praise and Claim monologues are stories about "positive" qualities. We refer to them in quotes as "negative" and "positive" monologues because of how they sound to others when they are spoken. Actually, all four monologues have similar effects on the development of relationships.

Note that monologues are a particular kind of statement. They are based on "either/or" logic and separate people into two groups, those who have certain characteristics and those who do not. Not all negative statements are monologues. If based in fact, the statement "Our income fell 15 percent last quarter because of a decline in sales in the western region" is simply a report about the company's financial status. It could be the basis for trying to increase sales. However, it could also become a negative monologue, used to blame others rather than to try to improve the situation.

Similarly, not all positive statements are monologues, either. If your organization was just recognized as one of the top places for people to work, you could justifiably celebrate the fact that "We're seen as one of the best." This statement would become a monologue only if it

led to boasting, lording it over others, acting superior, or feeling that there was nothing you could possibly learn from other organizations.

The "negative" monologues
Blame monologues focus on negative qualities that others have exhibited in the past. Some form of anger is associated with these monologues, though often in a masked or muted form, like frustration, irritation, or hurt. When we are focused on others' faults, we are distracted from seeing their strengths and contributions, and we are also not likely to see how we have contributed to the current situation.

> "There is nothing as easy as denouncing. It don't take much to see that something is wrong, but it takes some eyesight to see what will put it right again."—Will Rogers

Engaging to correct or control others' mistakes or faults is the usual reaction associated

"NEGATIVE" MONOLOGUES

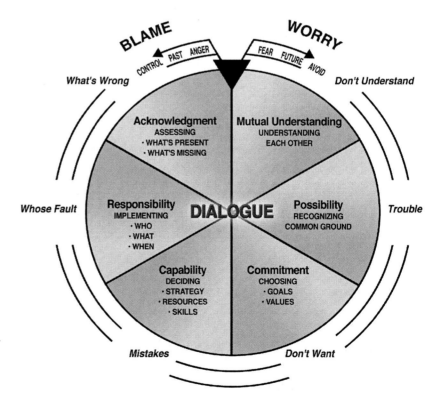

Blame monologues call attention to negative qualities of others

Based on a judgment (of others) *"Something's wrong."*	"What's going on? There are no notebooks for today's training program."
Assign responsibility *"It's X's (other's) fault."*	"I'll get to the bottom of this and find out whose fault it is. I'm sure it's the print shop."
Point to errors *"The mistake was . . ."*	"Can you believe it? The print shop let my request sit in their in box for three days. If they would check it every day, things like this wouldn't happen."
Focus on the "negative" *"I/We don't want that."*	"This can't ever happen again. I'm going to speak to the print shop supervisor."
Assume negative consequences *"The trouble with that is . . ."*	"How can they possibly think we can have programs without the notebooks? All the training programs will fail if this continues."
Declare understanding missing *"They don't understand."*	"How can they mess up so much and still keep their jobs? We'd get in trouble if we acted so irresponsibly."

with these monologues. Since Blame monologues are about others' faults, we frequently share our judgments with others, especially with those who have a similar view of the situation.

A Blame monologue flows counterclockwise around the outside of the Mobius Model diagram, beginning with Acknowledgment and ending with Mutual Understanding. Since this is a "negative" monologue, the language used sounds negative and is the counterpart to how it would sound if it were a dialogue.

In *Worry* monologues, we attribute negative qualities to ourselves and anticipate that these qualities will cause us difficulty at some point in the future. Some level of fear is usually associated with these monologues. Avoidance is a common reaction—we want to avoid revealing our inadequacies. Sometimes people say they are worried when they are actually blaming others for some deficiency. When we refer to Worry monologues, we mean judgments about our own deficiencies. Since they are about our own inadequacies, we

Worry monologues call attention to negative qualities of self

Declare understanding missing I/We *"don't understand."*	"I'm afraid I don't have what it will take to lead this team."
Assume negative consequences *"The trouble" with that is . . ."*	"If I become leader, I'll probably fall flat on my face, and we'll fail."
Focus on the "negative" *"I/We don't want that."*	"The team can't miss the target date—I'd be fired just like Joan was."
Point to (potential) errors *"The mistake was . . ."*	"How can I possibly do this? I don't know where to start; I don't know even the basics about being a team leader!"
Assign responsibility *"I'm afraid it will be my fault."*	"I've done what I can—posted the target dates in the break room and supplied everyone with planning forms."
Based on a judgment about self *"Something's wrong."*	"I tried, but I'm afraid I wasn't cut out to be a team leader."

often keep Worry monologues to ourselves, revealing them only to our closest confidants.

A Worry monologue flows clockwise around the outside of the Mobius Model diagram, beginning with Mutual Understanding and ending with Acknowledgment. Since this is a "negative" monologue, the language used sounds negative and is the counterpart to how it would sound if it were a dialogue.

The "positive" monologues

In a "positive" monologue, the language used sounds positive; however, it has the separating effect of putting one person or group above or below oneself or one's own group.

It may be surprising to learn that both of the positive monologues—Praise and Claim—can limit relationship development and the ability to reach shared goals. This is because all monologues distinguish individuals and groups from each other by attributing a quality to some individuals or groups but not to others. To say that

someone is brilliant and charismatic is to distinguish him or her from others who are not. When a distinguished speaker is introduced to an audience, the purpose of the introduction is to set the speaker apart as someone special that merits our attention. She is different from me in some praiseworthy way. On the other hand, if I introduced myself to someone in a way that calls attention to my special qualities, I may sound arrogant. Even if the brilliance and charisma of the speaker, or my own superior performance, is indisputable, saying so can get in the way of connecting effectively with others.

Praise monologues are about positive qualities we attribute to others and that we desire for ourselves. We appreciate those qualities and believe the future will be better if we associate with those who already have them. "The marketing team is world class; I wish our team were like theirs" is an example of a Praise statement.

Because Praise monologues are about the gifts or strengths of others, we usually don't hesitate to speak them, especially to those who agree with us (though we may be careful in sharing our thoughts and feelings directly with the CEO).

Claim monologues are about positive qualities I attribute to myself or my group and that set me or my group apart from others. These monologues call attention to past accomplishments. We are proud of what we have done and let others know by talking about accomplishments or virtues, or just by acting out of a sense of superiority. For example, "It's so obvious that we are the best team in this company" is a Claim statement. Other teams, lacking the qualities we have, ought to follow our example—we can show them the way. Often, Claim monologues are not shared comfortably with others but are kept as a private "truth" that acts to separate us from others. However, when we do share these monologues, it is to per-

"POSITIVE" MONOLOGUES

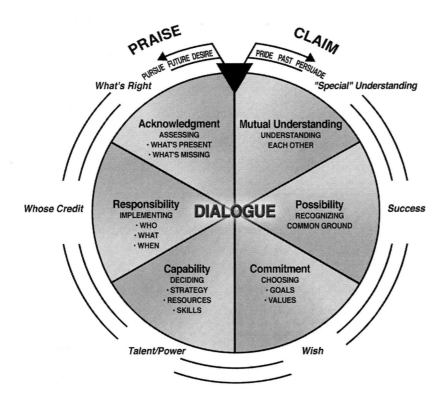

Praise monologues call attention to the talents or strengths of others

Begin with a judgment *"Something's right."*	"Profits are up!"
Give credit to others *"Credit belongs to . . ."*	"It's the new CEO."
Point out special capabilities *"Her/his special talents are . . ."*	"She's uniquely brilliant and charismatic."
Express a desire *"I wish . . ."*	"I want her to stay on as CEO as long as possible. I'd like to be on her team. I wish my boss were like her."
Envision success *"My image of success is . . ."*	"I want her to select me to be on her team."
"Special" understanding is attributed to I/you or we/they *"She/he understands . . ."*	"She is uniquely able to lead. There will never be another leader like her."

suade others to agree with us about our special qualities.

Once we become aware of our monologues, we have a choice. We can continue to act only on the basis of our thoughts and feelings and seek agreement or compliance from those who differ. Or, in dialogue, we can choose to share our point of view with others, listen to their points of view, and together discover what none of us can see alone. I can sit around wishing we were as good as the marketing team but thinking we are not. Or I can share my appreciation and my wish in dialogue with others so that together we can see new possibilities.

Dialogue

Dialogue is a conversation for development that leads to a qualitative improvement in our relationships with others. It can take place when people recognize and acknowledge that their differences are *joint* assets and differing strengths that contribute to the development of relationships.

We also refer to dialogue as *Creative Dialogue* because it helps create something (e.g., understanding, collaboration, an action plan) that didn't exist before the dialogue occurred. (It is described more fully in chapters 3 and 4.) Creative Dialogue begins with developing Mutual Understanding and flows clockwise around the Mobius Model,

Claim monologues call attention to my/our accomplishments and special qualities

Claim "special" understanding *"I understand . . ."*	"I know this industry inside and out."
Claim a unique potential *"I imagine success as . . ."*	"I can lead this organization to great success."
Want to make the potential visible *"I wish that . . ."*	"All I need is a chance to be heard by the whole organization."
Claim exceptional capabilities *"My special talents are . . ."*	"I am able to see the big picture that others can't."
Claim credit for self *"I deserve credit for . . ."*	"Under my leadership, my department has done great things."
Call attention to self *"I've got what it takes to . . ."*	"I'm the best one to do this job right."

culminating with Acknowledgment. For example, Creative Dialogue would be used if the members of a team held widely divergent views of what their priorities should be for the coming year and could not come to agreement about how to proceed with their annual planning.

In this dialogue, participants develop mutual understanding of

- Differences in their viewpoints
- Common ground about what is desirable
- Shared commitments to take action
- Collaborative ways to fulfill commitments
- Responsibilities for taking appropriate action
- Acknowledgment about what is present that contributes to the shared understanding and what is still missing

BASIC TOOLS FOR DIALOGUE

Three basic tools of dialogue—listening for, speaking for, and acknowledging Mutual Understanding—are described here. In the descriptions, the focus is on Mutual Understanding; however, these tools are essential at each step of the Mobius process. When there is a dialogue to create Possibility, reaching mutual understanding of each participant's point of view about "What's possible?" is fundamental. When there is dialogue for Commitment, it is similarly important to reach common understanding of the commitments that are being made. In the same manner, these tools are used during the Capability, Responsibility, and Acknowledgment phases of dialogue. After these tools have been described, Barb and Laura's situation (introduced in chapter 1) will be used to illustrate their application.

How to Listen and Speak for Mutual Understanding

You probably don't need to be convinced that Mutual Understanding is better than misunderstanding, conflict, or a silent standoff. The real question is what do you have to do to make it happen, especially when people are already upset? How long does it have to take? What if the other person doesn't want to understand?

You may agree, in theory, with the basic assumptions of the Mobius Model:

- Mutual Understanding is an important first step in all relationship development.
- Relationship development is a natural process that is fueled by differences—positive and negative.
- Disagreement and confusion are good times to choose to have a dialogue.

But you may still wonder if, in practice, choosing to do what it takes to get to Mutual Understanding is always worth it—especially when it may take too long or seem too upsetting.

If you choose to get to Mutual Understanding, the few simple rules outlined below will be helpful. They are easy to understand but more difficult to follow. By increasing your skill in the ways of speaking and listening described below, both the time and the difficulty are dramatically decreased.

What does Mutual Understanding mean?

Mutual Understanding *does not* mean agreement with each other's viewpoints—this is a very important point. Most resistance to listening occurs because we are afraid we will be heard as agreeing with something when we don't. But Mutual Understanding *does* mean agreement about what each other's actual viewpoints are. The diagram on page 17 identifies three areas in which two or more participants may agree or disagree about their viewpoints.

Mutual Understanding means that participants agree about A, B, and C.

If you are like many others, the most difficult part of getting to Mutual Understanding is listening to others when you passionately disagree about something. One natural reaction is to assume that they don't understand and to speak to them about what they don't understand. Another natural reaction is to hide your real point of view—"Maybe I don't understand something important here!" Both reactions are natural, but neither lead to creative dialogue.

How does a dialogue for Mutual Understanding work? A dialogue is a conversation in which participants agree to *add* each other's point of view to their own viewpoint. The assumption underlying dialogue is that, as we add other viewpoints than our own, we will begin to recognize a bigger picture than we understood before—we will find the common ground C. There is no attempt to change anyone's viewpoint. Viewpoints will change as a natural result of new understanding.

The key steps in a dialogue for Mutual Understanding are outlined

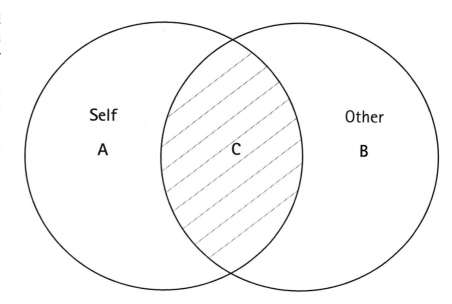

A and B represent places where each person's viewpoint differs with the other. C represents common ground where viewpoints do agree.

below, along with some tips for improving your skills. Dialogue requires skills in both listening and speaking, but it isn't rocket science. Making the choice to enter into dialogue is always the biggest challenge. We know it's good for us to exercise, but do we do it? It's productive to enter into dialogue when you have a difference with someone. Will you do it?

Used with commitment and skill, the following rules for speaking and listening can lead to Mutual Understanding. You can begin as the speaker or the listener. It doesn't matter. What does matter is the intention to understand and learn.

Listening to understand

What can you do if someone says something that you disagree with strongly, and you want to begin a dialogue? You can *listen to understand* and put aside, for the moment, your need to tell the other that you disagree.

1. Acknowledge that you may not *yet* fully understand the others' viewpoint, and that you want to understand.
2. Ask the others to continue sharing their thoughts and feelings about the current topic, issue, or situation, especially what they are not yet sure you understand.
3. When the speaker seems finished, or after she or he makes several key points that you think you understand, say:
   a. "I would like to tell you what I think I understand so far and then ask you to
      - Correct me where I didn't get it quite right, and
      - Add whatever else you think I need to know."
   b. If the speaker suggests changes to, or expands on, what you said, *be sure* to reflect your understanding of what the others think or feel. State the changes or additions using their language.
   c. If the speaker keeps repeating a point, it means you do not seem, to the speaker, to be understanding; change your way of saying what you hear until the speaker indicates that you "get it."

4. When the speaker indicates that you get it, ask, "Is there anything else I need to know to understand your point of view?"

5. Repeat steps 3 and 4 until each speaker indicates that she or he thinks you understand, and then ask to add your own point of view (see Speaking to Be Understood, below).

Tips for listening to understand

• Never say, "I understand"; say what you think you understand to see if the speaker agrees that you get it. Saying "I understand" when the other person doesn't think you do can be infuriating.

• If you know you don't understand something a speaker says, ask for clarification: "I'm not sure I understood what you meant when you said . . ." But be sure your question is sincere and not a challenge to their point of view.

• Don't ask for clarification about what *you* see as unwanted implications of what someone says; you are more likely to be understood if you wait until the other thinks that you understand their point of view.

• Don't say, "I agree (or disagree)." Clarifying agreements and disagreements in viewpoints comes *after* the other says you get it. Saying that you agree or disagree takes attention off the speaker's point of view and focuses it on your point of view.

Speaking to be understood

What do you do when your own point of view differs from what others are saying, and you are not sure they really want to understand? You can *speak to be understood.* The important point is to remember that you want a dialogue that leads to Mutual Understanding, not agreement. Agreement will flow from Mutual Understanding.

Try taking the following steps, especially if others haven't had a chance to speak yet:

1. Acknowledge that you are not sure that you understand the others' viewpoint, and you want to.

2. Identify what you anticipate will be key points of agreement (C) and, briefly, outline that common ground.

3. Respectfully acknowledge the points you heard the others make about which you may disagree, and repeat that you want to understand their viewpoint once you have finished speaking.

4. Explain the thoughts and feelings you most want others to understand (A).

5. Say that you would be happy to respond to questions of clarification if there are any.

6. Then, listen to understand and add other viewpoints to your own.

Tips for speaking to be understood

• When you describe the parts of your viewpoint that differ from the others (A), especially if you have already listened to understand, begin by, briefly, acknowledging the viewpoints of previous speaker(s).

• Focus on what you think others may not yet understand about your viewpoint.

• When answering questions of clarification, first acknowledge what they got right and then focus on what you think they may not yet understand.

How to Acknowledge Mutual Understanding
When is a dialogue for Mutual Understanding complete?

Mutual Understanding about an issue or situation is complete when participants acknowledge that their viewpoints have been understood by each other (all agree about A, B, and C in the figure on page 17). Of course, two people never fully understand each other about everything. That is why we are an infinite resource for each other to expand our ways of understanding and interacting.

It is important to take a moment, when some-one feels Mutual Understanding is present, to check in with each other. A brief go-round to hear from everyone about the following two questions is a good way to assess satisfaction with the dialogue and bring it to a close:

- What key things do I understand now that I didn't before the dialogue?
- Are there any new possibilities I want to explore further?

Once Mutual Understanding is present, there is a natural movement from Mutual Understanding to recognizing common ground for exploring new possibilities.

BARB AND LAURA'S CREATIVE DIALOGUE

In chapter 1, we introduced Barb and Laura, who seemed to be stymied by their different approaches to jointly planning an upcoming conference. Let's assume that Laura has recently learned about the tools for dialogue and is willing to give them a try.

LAURA: Barb, you know I've been avoiding the planning meetings you've called.

BARB (a bit sarcastically): Yeah, I noticed.

LAURA (taking a deep breath): I know you want to make a detailed plan now, before we do any-thing else, and I was wondering if we could talk for a few minutes about that. I'd like to under-stand why you think it is important to plan in detail now.

BARB: If you really want to know, I think we'll end up in a big mess unless we make some good plans now to guide us.

LAURA: It's important not to end up in a big mess, for sure. I know we both want it to be a great conference. I'd like to hear about how you think planning in detail now could help us avoid that.

BARB: If you don't get plans locked in early, people will just drag out the planning and not reach agreement, and the situation will get out of control. We have to decide the three main content tracks for the conference, and who the speakers will be, as soon as possible so that the speakers can make plans and we can get the best airfares and housing. If we don't plan now, when it becomes my job to take care of all the details like handouts and food arrangements—as I know it will—I'll end up rushing around at the end and not getting the best deals.

LAURA: You want us to get good speakers early enough that we can get economical airfares and housing for them. You also want to be sure who-ever is handling the handouts, food arrange-ments, and other necessary details has time to get good-quality, economical deals. You think that you are probably the one who will end up in the role of managing the details. Have I under-stood your point of view?

BARB: Yeah, that's what usually happens. No one else wants to manage the details; do you?

LAURA: Well, let me tell you where I agree with you and offer some other thoughts, and then we can look together at who will do what. I agree that we want to have good quality and get good deals on all the necessary arrangements, and to do that we need to plan in a timely way. I want us to divide the responsibilities in a fair way so that neither of us is stuck with work that we don't want to do or are not good at. I think our inter-ests and skills may be complementary.

I'm reluctant to agree to a set agenda right now because I will be attending a conference in New York in two weeks, and I know that some of the people attending are potential speakers for our conference. I would like to speak with them about their current research and interests in our field and let them know about our conference. I think that after conversations with them, we would have a better idea about how to plan. It is important to me that we agree on ways to take advantage of opportunities for the conference as they emerge while still maintaining quality and economy.

BARB: So you think we can get some good speakers at the conference you are going to in two weeks?

LAURA: Yes.

BARB: Well, it would be great if you could get Dr. Ono and Phyllis Black. Will they be there? Do you think you could get them?

LAURA: Yes, I was thinking of them and two others. So, I would like to wait a few weeks until I have those conversations, and some follow-up conversations, before we finalize the program. If we were able to agree to a program by March 1, would that give us enough time to make good-quality, economic arrangements?

BARB: Well, that would be great if you could get them. Yes, March 1 will give us time to get arrangements made, but we must have final content agreed to by then. If you get the speakers and manage the content, I would be glad to make proposals for travel and food arrangements. I will need your support to implement the plans.

LAURA: I agree to finalize the content by March 1, and I am delighted that you will manage the food and travel arrangements. I look forward to your proposals and will provide support. Other opportunities may arise, so we need to communicate clearly and frequently with each other to be sure we agree to timelines to get results we both want.

BARB: Okay, let's plan a meeting right after you return from New York so we can be sure to be ready to move by March 1. And let's plan to meet for at least an hour every week after that so you can keep me informed as you see new possibilities we should consider.

LAURA: Great, this could be fun. I really respect your ability to manage the timelines and the crucial details.

BARB: Yeah, thanks for talking with me about this. I think we'll make a good team.

SUMMARY

This chapter provides a guide for recognizing your monologues and for taking the first steps to bring them into dialogue. It also points out the specific sequence of steps to get to mutually satisfying results. Chapter 3 provides a detailed road map to guide the conversation after the first crucial step into dialogue. Chapter 4 provides examples of applications of Creative Dialogue.

Monologue and Dialogue in a Nutshell

	In a Monologue	In a Dialogue
Basic dynamic	I/we express and defend my/our point of view as the truth (though in actuality it is just that part of the truth that my/our unique experience makes known to us). Monologues invite agreement or argument.	Everyone's point of view is shared, understood, and added to others' so that partial truths are combined. Together, we discover what none of us can see alone. In dialogue, nothing is lost, and new, unexpected potential is revealed.
Relationships among people	People are separated from one another by being divided into one group, which has particular qualities, and another that lacks those qualities. This leads to I/you or we/they thinking and talking that limits the development of relationships.	Understanding differences and combining viewpoints leads to discovering common ground and expands the ways a relationship may grow: "I might think and do the same thing in their place."
Time orientation	Focusing on the past or the future hinders relationship development by distracting us from the present moment to pay attention to past events or future concerns.	Focusing on the present (where the only real opportunity for change exists) creates opportunities for actions that grow the relationship.
Type of logic	An either/or logic distinguishes self from other or us from them.	A both/and logic includes everyone and values and encompasses all viewpoints.
Impulse to act	We are stimulated to • avoid expressing our own inadequacies • fight so we can correct others' deficiencies • profess our own virtues, or • pursue the qualities we believe we lack.	We are stimulated to engage in a dialogue and listen to understand others.

» » » » »

CHAPTER THREE

Using the Mobius Model as a Road Map for Creative Dialogue

A good map makes it easier to find your way in new territory. Although it doesn't guarantee that you won't get lost, it does provide a way for you to recognize that you are lost and to show you how to circle back to find your route. It also illustrates how to read signs and indicates tools that can be useful at points along the way. This is what the Mobius Model provides when you want to navigate new territory using Creative Dialogue.

THE FLOW OF A CREATIVE DIALOGUE

The Creative Dialogue moves clockwise around the Mobius Model, beginning with Mutual Understanding and culminating with Acknowledgment. It is used in situations where people want different things, and their differences are an obstacle to collaboration. The presence of a "negative" monologue, blame or worry, is often an indicator that a Creative Dialogue is called for.

This section details the flow of a Creative Dialogue, providing, for each quality, indicators of when it is present or missing, a team example, and tools and approaches for creating it.

MUTUAL UNDERSTANDING

Mutual Understanding means each person is understood and understands the others. It is present when each person confirms that she or he feels understood by and also understands everyone else.

When it is present, people will say what they really think or feel about the subject of the conversation. They value and learn from the differences among themselves. When others speak, they listen and expect to learn.

When Mutual Understanding is missing, people feel misunderstood and disrespected, and they don't trust each other. Differences among people are ignored or become the cause of disagreements. People are reluctant to say what they really think or feel, and they may keep relevant information to themselves. They expect others to listen to and learn from them, but they themselves do not expect to listen to or learn from others.

Tools for Creating Mutual Understanding

Listening and speaking for understanding have already been presented as the basic tools for bringing about Mutual Understanding. This kind of listening contrasts with interactions in which we do things such as give feedback or advocate for a particular course of action. The cartoon at the bottom of the following page by Lynn Johnston clearly illustrates the differences among these ways of engaging with others.

What happened in this cartoon is a common occurrence: We enter into a conversation thinking that all parties are on the same wavelength only to discover that some are on AM and others FM, that some expect to be heard and listened to while others are expecting to give advice or offer solutions.

A Team with Mutual Understanding Present

On our team, we work hard to make sure that we understand one another. We know that each of us brings an important, different perspective and that we will have a better understanding of each issue or situation if we listen carefully to each other. We also want each individual to know that he or she is understood because this contributes to the overall well-being and effectiveness of the team. We remind each other that you can understand others without necessarily agreeing with them.

When there's some kind of misunderstanding (which might be about people's thoughts, feelings, or actions), we listen carefully, say back what we hear others communicating, and have the speaker confirm that he or she has been understood. It's not always easy to do this, but we keep at it and take the time necessary because putting our heads together to reach joint understanding is fundamental to our success and saves us a lot of time in the long run. When people know that the team has listened to their point of view and information, then they are situated to do their best work.

When we achieve this kind of understanding, we usually come to see our situation in a new way; we start to trust each other more and share our ideas more openly. These can become the basis for a genuinely shared vision.

When listening for understanding, we seek to contribute to Mutual Understanding by listening, taking in and appreciating the information and perspective contained in others' points of view, and then saying what our understanding is to confirm that we have understood.

When we engage in this kind of conversation, we expect to be understood by the others, but not necessarily agreed with. We expect to learn, and we specifically do not do the following:

- Disagree *or* agree with others
- Commiserate with them
- Offer advice or solutions
- Promote or defend our own position
- Tell a similar story of our own

For many people, particularly in settings where taking action to get results is highly valued, staying engaged in listening in this way is very challenging. We want to have our say.

Different kinds of conversations are needed for developing effective and satisfying relationships. In working and living together, things work out better when we reach understanding of others before setting goals, planning, and taking action that we expect others to commit to as well. In the Mobius Model, reaching understanding of one another occurs before these other activities because it provides the underpinning for them. However, moving through and completing each phase of the Mobius process is essential to having a truly creative dialogue.

For Better or For Worse®   by Lynn Johnston

Used with permission of the author

Relationship of Mutual Understanding to Possibility and Acknowledgment

In the flow of the Mobius Model, Mutual Understanding is preceded by Acknowledgment and leads into Possibility.

Acknowledgment involves recognition of what has been accomplished and what is still missing in order for current commitments to be fulfilled. People's differing views of what is present and missing at the conclusion of the previous conversation are a natural beginning point for the next one. In this way, Acknowledgment feeds forward to initiate a new conversation for Mutual Understanding and another creative dialogue.

Mutual Understanding is the beginning of a creative conversation. Fully understanding all viewpoints can reveal previously unrecognized common ground. This common ground is the

Mutual Understanding in a Nutshell

Mutual Understanding exists when each person says she or he is understood and also understands the others. (Note that Mutual Understanding is not the same as mutual agreement. One can understand others without necessarily agreeing with them.)

When This Quality Is Present, People	When This Quality Is Missing, People	During This Step, People	Tools and Approaches	If This Step Is Skipped or Left Incomplete, People Might	Indicators of Readiness to Move to the Next Step
Feel understood, respected. Will say what they really think or feel about the subject of the conversation. Value and learn from differences. Expect to listen to and learn from others.	Express disrespect for others and other viewpoints. Distrust others and are reluctant to express their real thoughts and feelings. Discount viewpoints that differ from their own. Offer flattery and insincere positive opinions.	Acknowledge their different viewpoints. Dialogue about their differing perceptions and viewpoints so that they understand their situation in a new way. Gain new perspectives on the current situation that lead to seeing new possibilities.	Check-in Listening for Mutual Understanding Speaking for Mutual Understanding	Complain that others don't understand, that no one listens to them. Insist that others "go first" in demonstrating that they understand. May refuse to speak (because "they" wouldn't understand) or to listen (because "they" won't be honest).	People are surprised to find that they agree more than they thought they did and want to see if they can discover even more common ground. There is a growing sense of hope and connection with others.

Transition Question:

Does anyone have anything to add, that you are not sure all of us understand yet, that would be important for us to understand about (this issue/topic)?

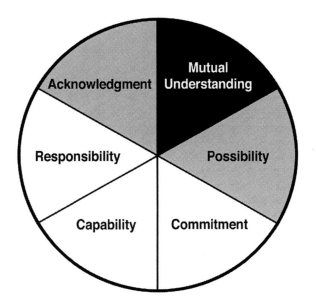

basis for discovering new possibilities. Without this understanding, possibilities are difficult to recognize; sometimes we don't want them to work out if we can't get the respect we feel we deserve first.

POSSIBILITY

Possibility means everyone recognizes that there is something desirable that could be created through collaboration.

When Possibility is present, people focus on what they want to create, not what they want to avoid. They welcome new ideas, see challenges as opportunities, and discuss and respect differences without attacking people. They proceed from the belief that things can be made better, that challenges can be met, and that issues can be resolved.

When Possibility is missing, people focus on what they want to avoid. They are not interested in and may resist new ideas, and they are reluctant to make suggestions because they fear their proposals will get shot down. They believe that there is little or no possibility of making things better, meeting challenges, resolving issues, or being understood. They are often deeply invested in defending their point of view that things can't get better.

Tools for Creating Possibility

When considering new possibilities for their situation, it is common for people to begin by focusing on what's wrong. Shifting "what's wrong" statements into descriptions of "what's missing" is a key approach to creating Possibility. This shift in a conversation for Possibility is comparable to listening for understanding in a conversation for Mutual Understanding and can be equally challenging to initiate and sustain.

For example, "What's really wrong around here is that no one cares if we do a good job or not!" is a "what's wrong" statement. To transform this statement, ask, "What's missing that, if it were present, would make this an attractive situation to you?" The complaint about no one caring might be restated, "What's missing is acknowledging what we've accomplished when we reach our goals."

Since speaking this way is new to many

A Team with Possibility Present

Our team is known as an exciting team to be on because we believe we can make things better. We see challenging situations as hidden opportunities that are best approached by finding another way of understanding the situation. We do this by exploring our different viewpoints until we identify common ground, and by staying focused on what we want to create together (not what is wrong or what we want to avoid or control).

We welcome new ideas and ways to do things because we don't have many sacred cows and like to consider better ways to work together and accomplish our goals. We don't get distracted by evaluating whether to take a particular action until we have challenged ourselves to think outside the box. We are able to explore each other's thinking respectfully, assuming we will learn something.

We establish a vision shared by all team members before moving ahead. By the time a new idea is adopted, everyone is behind it and feels a sense of ownership.

Possibility in a Nutshell

Possibility exists when everyone recognizes that something desirable could be created through collaboration.

When This Quality Is Present, People	When This Quality Is Missing, People	During This Step, People	Tools and Approaches	If This Step Is Skipped or Left Incomplete, People Might	Indicators of Readiness to Move to the Next Step
Welcome new ideas and see challenges as opportunities. Discuss and respect different ideas without attacking others. Focus on what they want to create (not on what they don't want). Believe that things can be made better, that their problems can be overcome.	Debunk others' beliefs as naïve and uninformed. Regard others' proposals as unrealistic. Affirm or pretend belief in the face of grave doubts. Go along with another's fantasy as if it were real.	Develop new understanding of the situation, leads to seeing possibilities where there were none before. Become clear about what it is they want to create together.	Asking "What if?" For example, "What if we could get the resources?" Shifting "what's wrong" stories into descriptions of "what's missing." Mind mapping	Call attention to what they don't want, problems, and issues. Think and speak about problems or issues in either/or terms, assuming that if others gain they will lose. Declare creative resolutions impossible.	There's newly recognized common ground that can be the basis for moving ahead together. There's a call for action. There's a growing sense of hope and renewed energy and enthusiasm.

Transition Question:

If all the conditions we've listed (or mentioned) were present,
would there be anything still missing for you to be fully satisfied?

people, there may be silence or a little confusion when "what's missing" is asked for the first time. However, with patience and encouragement, people soon begin to recognize the benefits of thinking and talking this way.

When trying to imagine new possibilities, people may note the obstacles they see, the reasons why "it" wouldn't be possible. When this happens, asking "What if?" can help move the focus from seeing barriers to perceiving new opportunities. For example, in response to the statement "We don't have enough resources to do anything creative around here," ask, "What would we see if we could get the resources?"

Simply listing the possibilities that people identify and mind mapping are other tools that can be used to create Possibility.

Relationship of Possibility to Mutual Understanding and Commitment

In the flow of the Mobius Model, Possibility leads into Commitment and is preceded by Mutual Understanding.

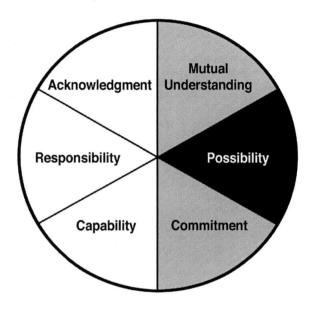

Possibility flows naturally from the new awareness that is created through Mutual Understanding. Because people "see" things that they didn't see before and acknowledge common ground where they had thought none existed, they now perceive possibilities that previously would have been dismissed as nonexistent, unnecessary, or impractical.

Recognition of new possibilities paves the way for Commitment because something that is both desirable and feasible is now acknowledged. Compliance or "go-along" behavior, not true Commitment, occurs when people are asked to undertake an effort they do not see as advantageous or realistic, one that they do not view as possible.

COMMITMENT

Commitment means that there is agreement to priorities among the goals and values that will direct action toward making possibilities real. Goals are circumstances intended to exist at some specific time in the future. Values are conditions that we want to exist at all times in our relationship.

There are three basic statements of Commitment: yes, no, and I'll let you know at a specific time in the future.

When Commitment is present, goals and values are spelled out and agreed on *before* taking action. These desired results are then used to direct action, allocate resources, and measure progress and success.

When Commitment is missing, people are not clear about and may not share the same goals and values. So they may be working toward disparate ends, or toward no particular goals or values at all. Unable to agree about priorities, they lack a clear basis for measuring success.

Tools for Creating Commitment

Three questions are the primary tools for creating Commitment.

A Team with Commitment Present

This team is clear about our goals and values—what we are trying to accomplish and the conditions we want to characterize us as a team. We share a vision of what success looks like for the next year, and we start by deliberately identifying what we want to result from our actions. (Later, we spell out the particular steps we need to take.) We are just as clear about the values that guide our actions. We focus our daily work on achieving the end results while maintaining our values. We use the goals and values to gauge whether or not we are on track.

When people say yes or no, they really mean it and expect to be held accountable.

When we're clear about our desired goals and values, then we're ready to make a plan for how to accomplish them.

Commitment in a Nutshell

Commitment exists when the goals, values, and priorities that will guide action have been chosen.
- Goals are formulated in terms of measurable conditions that will be present at a specific time in the future.
- Values are conditions desired to exist at all times in a relationship.

When This Quality Is Present, People	When This Quality Is Missing, People	During This Step, People	Tools and Approaches	If This Step Is Skipped or Left Incomplete, People Might	Indicators of Readiness to Move to the Next Step
Spell out and agree on goals and values before taking action. Direct their actions and resources toward a prioritized set of common goals and values. Use goals, values, and priorities to measure success.	Attribute negative intentions to others' proposed goals and values. Waffle about their own point of view. Hide their real intentions from others. Give lip service to the aspirations of others.	State a broad possibility in terms of the values and measurable goals that will direct action for a specific period of time. Establish priorities.	*Regarding a proposed action:* Ask: "So that what?" (i.e., "You want to do ___ so that ___would result?") *Regarding unwanted results or actions:* Ask: "What would that look like by ___ time?" Ask: "Is anything still missing in our goals and values for you to be satisfied?" Priority-setting and decision-making techniques	Put a positive spin on their own intentions and a negative one on the intention of others. Assume the role of only being a critic, not making positive proposals or suggestions for improvement. Evaluate proposals only in terms of the impact on their own interests.	People are clear about and committed to their goals, values, and priorities, but do not yet know how to accomplish them. There is a shared vision of what success would look like.

Transition Question:

If these results were present by (time), would anything else still be missing for you to be satisfied?

Commitment brings the focus to desired results; actions to achieve those results are considered later. However, at this point, some people jump to proposing actions, e.g., "Let's have a team-building retreat." When someone proposes an action before the desired results have been identified, ask, "So that what? You want to have a team-building retreat so that what would will result?"

Sometimes it is necessary to ask this question more than once. The person who proposed the team-building retreat might say, "We should have a retreat so we can all get together." Getting together is also an activity, and the question can be posed again: "We should all get together so that what would result?"

"It would be good if we understood each other better. We all have different ways of communicating, and when we have a problem, our different ways of communicating just seem to make it worse. I would like a better understanding of how to work more smoothly when we disagree and have conflict."

Note that "So that what?" could also be asked about the desire to work together more smoothly. "You want to work together more smoothly so that what would result?" However, the questioning stops once people agree that a desirable result has been identified.

Another common response is to focus on what is not wanted rather than what is wanted. For example, "I wish we'd stop all this arguing and bickering" reflects what is *not* wanted. To transform this statement into a possible goal, ask, "What would it look like if ___ were gone?" i.e., "What would it look like if the arguing and bickering stopped?" In this situation, a statement of what is wanted would be, "Well, if we didn't argue and disagree so much, it would be more pleasant to work here, and we'd get more work done."

The third question for creating Commitment is, "Is anything still missing in our goals and values for you to be satisfied?" This query is intended to assure that the final statement of goals and values includes what is important to each person.

In addition, various priority-setting and decision-making techniques can be used in creating Commitment.

Relationship of Commitment to Possibility and Capability

In the flow of the Mobius Model, Commitment leads into Capability and is preceded by Possibility.

Possibility sets the stage for a conversation for Commitment by providing shared understanding of something desirable and feasible to create collaboratively. In Commitment, this generally defined possibility is refined into goals and values to direct action. *What* will be created is spelled out.

Commitment clarifies the current priorities among the goals and values. Once these choices have been made, it is natural to ask *how* the commitments can be carried out. The work of Capability is to create a way to fulfill commitments and to garner the necessary resources. Trying to plan before everyone reaches a common commitment leads to focusing on activities rather than clear results and can result in dissipation of resources.

CAPABILITY

Capability means that people have agreed how to combine knowledge, skills, and resources in innovate ways that enable all commitments to be met.

When Capability is present, people believe that they have—or can develop—a way to meet any challenge. They are willing to try, to learn from their mistakes, and to incorporate what they learn into current and future efforts. They like to roll up their sleeves and bring new ideas to life.

When Capability is missing, people are less interested in, and may resist, trying new things because they think things are okay the way they are, or they are afraid of making mistakes. They may feel incapable of making things better.

A Team with Capability Present

We are a team that makes things happen because we're serious about finding a way to realize the goals and values we've chosen. We have a good track record for sticking with projects until they bear fruit. Before taking specific actions, we make the effort to determine how our commitments can be realized and to agree on a plan we believe will work.

When we don't know what to do, we're confident that, by pooling our different strengths, we can come up with a way to meet any challenge. Learning new ways is encouraged, and adopting new ideas is a key to how we work.

Once we've settled on a feasible plan, then we're ready to clarify what specifically needs to happen to carry out the plan.

Tools for Creating Capability

Creating Capability entails determining how best to realize the goals and values that have been committed to, as well as garnering the resources (such as authority, knowledge, skills, funding, equipment, and space) needed to attain them. It is essentially a planning phase, whether formal or casual, and it relies on tools such as force field analysis, decision matrix, and brainstorming. Many other deliberate approaches to planning can also be used.

As in the development of the other qualities of relationship, members of groups bring a diversity of talents, knowledge, skills, and resources to the challenge of creating effective new Capabilities. The many technical tools available to groups become most effective when they are put to work in conversations that draw on the existing strengths of the members. Real synergy in a group requires that tools like brainstorming and force field analysis be used in a way that allows the unique talents, knowledge, and skills of each member to be brought into play. This means group conversations that include times of suspended judgment to encourage divergent and offbeat ideas that may spark surprising new thoughts. It also requires times of convergent, group decision-making, in which the "best" way is selected on the basis of criteria to which members have agreed.

Relationship of Capability to Commitment and Responsibility

In the flow of the Mobius Model, Capability leads into Responsibility and is preceded by Commitment.

Commitment sets the stage for Capability by clar-

ifying the priority goals and values that will be pursued. During Commitment, the focus is deliberately kept on desired results, postponing consideration of how those results might be achieved. Capability provides a way of acting and the resources required to carry out the commitments.

Spelling out and agreeing to a plan sets the stage for Responsibility, where specific action steps and timelines are delineated, and individuals or units commit to completing actions. A plan is just an idea until agreements are made about who will take what actions by when.

Capability in a Nutshell

Capability exists when there is agreement to a way that will lead to fulfilling all commitments.

When This Quality Is Present, People	When This Quality Is Missing, People	During This Step, People	Tools and Approaches	If this Step Is Skipped or Left Incomplete, People Might	Indicators of Readiness to Move to the Next Step
Rise to new challenges. Are willing to do "what it takes"; are confident that together they can meet the challenge. Identify and acquire the resources and training they need. View mistakes as part of learning.	Call attention to past defects and failures in a proposed way to do something. Express lack of confidence in any change effort. Brag and exaggerate confidence in their own abilities. Dismiss or ignore the concerns and criticisms of others.	Determine what to do to achieve the commitments and formulate an approach that everyone agrees will work. Needed resources (such as authority, knowledge, skills, money, equipment, and space) are identified.	Ask: "How will we realize the goals and values to which we have just committed?" Force field analysis Brainstorming Alternative selection matrix Other deliberate approaches to planning	Insist that others come up with solutions to problems and issues. Point to inadequate resources and training to explain poor results.	A way to meet all commitments has been agreed to. People are ready to figure out what specifically will have to happen in order for commitments to be met.

Transition Question:

Is there anything missing for you to be confident that we could take these (listed) actions, using these (listed) resources, and get the results we want?

RESPONSIBILITY

Responsibility means that everyone knows who is going to do what by when; it is the carrying out of the plan to meet the commitments.

When it is present, people know what they are expected to do—and what others are to do—and they do it. As individuals and as a group, they find satisfaction in doing a good job. And they talk openly about it if something doesn't get done. Even though responsibilities have been spelled out and committed to, people's tasks are not set in stone or inflexible. Responsibilities can be established anew when the situation changes, and people willingly work outside their specific responsibilities when they help someone else.

When Responsibility is missing, people are not clear about what they are expected to do, and so all the things necessary to carrying out the plan don't get done. People don't always do their part.

A Team with Responsibility Present

Our team is known as one that gets the job done and is on top of things—and we are. The people on our team know what they are supposed to do and can be counted on to do what they say they will do to carry out their commitments. That is because we take time, especially when we're beginning a new project, to clarify and agree on responsibilities and expectations and to confirm our next steps.

Though we're serious, we're not rigid, and we are willing to change assignments and take on new roles when there seems to be a better way to achieve the results we're after. We support one another in being responsible and pitch in wherever we're needed when we can. We talk it over as a team whenever responsibilities cannot be completed as we originally planned.

We recognize the importance of taking time to evaluate whether or not we accomplish the goals we set and if we have maintained our values in the process.

Responsibility in a Nutshell

Responsibility exists when there is agreement to expectations about who will do what by when to carry out the commitments.

When This Quality Is Present, People	When This Quality Is Missing, People	During This Step, People	Tools and Approaches	If This Step Is Skipped or Left Incomplete, People Might	Indicators of Readiness to Move to the Next Step
Are clear about what everyone has agreed to do. Agree to do their part. Agree to keep each other informed of results. Get things done, are "on top of things." Talk it over together when expectations aren't met.	Accuse others of not meeting expectations. Make excuses for not meeting expectations themselves. Defend their own behavior in the face of criticism. Ignore evidence and criticisms of failure to meet expectations.	Take time to clarify what is expected and to specify who will do what by when in order to carry out the commitments.	Action planning (Note that forms and procedures to record and track agreed-to responsibilities already exist in many organizations.)	Do only what is requested or required even if they know a better way. Do only what is formally spelled out, e.g., in their job description or contract.	Action is flowing naturally from having clear expectations and accountability. There is definite progress in carrying out the plan. People want to know "How are we doing?"

Transition Questions:

Is everyone clear and in agreement about who is expected to do what by when? Do you agree to do your part?

When something does fall through the cracks, it is either not talked about or is pointed out in a way in which the "irresponsible" party is blamed. There isn't an effort to see how the problem situation could be handled differently going forward.

Tools for Creating Responsibility

Planning and monitoring actions are the basic tools for creating Responsibility. Action planning is a common activity for many teams and individuals. The forms and procedures to record and track agreed-to responsibilities that are used in many organizations can be used during the Responsibility phase.

Relationship of Responsibility to Capability and Acknowledgment

In the flow of the Mobius Model, Responsibility leads into Acknowledgment and is preceded by Capability.

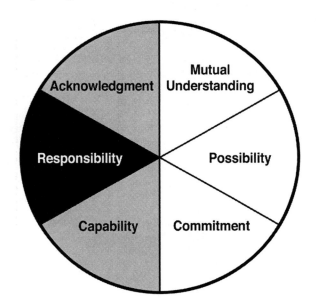

Creating Capability provides a particular approach to reach the commitments that were made, but it does not spell out specific steps. During the Responsibility phase, the particular actions necessary to carry out the plan are specified and taken by those who agree to be responsible. This is the implementation phase in formal planning processes.

As responsibilities are carried out, people nat-

urally want to take a look at what has resulted, to ask, "How are we doing?" Asking and responding to that question is the core of Acknowledgment, where considering what has been achieved and what still remains to be done is the focus.

ACKNOWLEDGMENT

Acknowledgment is recognizing what has been accomplished in terms of reaching the commitments and what remains to be done for the commitments to be complete, for the priority goals and values to be realized.

When it is present, both individuals and the whole group know where there is agreement and where there are differing perceptions about how well things are going and what still needs attention. Differing perceptions are openly accepted and considered, and there is a willingness to move ahead and address those things seen as missing.

When Acknowledgment is missing, people may not know how they are doing, even if they are doing quite well. This may be because they do not take time to consider this, they are not aware that there are differing views of the status quo, or they are reluctant to have divergent views expressed and given a full hearing. Individuals may be concerned about speaking up and can feel unacknowledged for their efforts and contributions.

A Team with Acknowledgment Present

We regularly take time to ask ourselves what's going well and what do we need to do differently, so we almost always know how we're doing in terms of realizing our chosen goals and values. We take this process seriously and freely share our differing viewpoints because being clear about how we all are doing and how each of us is doing increases our satisfaction and effectiveness.

We acknowledge each other's contributions and expect one another to say what we honestly think when we see something missing that is needed for our commitments to be complete.

We celebrate what we've accomplished, while the things we note are missing become the impetus for a new dialogue and plans for further action.

Tools for Creating Acknowledgment

The basic tools for creating Acknowledgment are three questions, the first of which asks what has resulted from the work so far, the second asks what still needs to be done, and the third asks where future efforts should be directed. The criteria for responding can be both objective and subjective, or experiential. For example, if producing a training manual were someone's responsibility, we can see whether or not it exists. On the other hand, if increasing the acknowledgment of people's contributions were the goal, we

Acknowledgment in a Nutshell

Acknowledgment exists when there is mutual recognition of what has been accomplished and what is still missing for the commitments to be fully realized.

When This Quality Is Present, People	When This Quality Is Missing, People	During This Step, People	Tools and Approaches	If This Step Is Skipped or Left Incomplete, People Might	Indicators of Readiness to Initiate Another Round of Dialogue
Know how well things are going. Feel free to share their differing perceptions. Recognize where there is agreement and disagreement about what is present and still missing. Are ready to continue to dialogue about remaining differences.	Belittle the efforts and results of others. Hide negative results. Exaggerate the positive outcomes of their own efforts. Discount their own negative results and the positive results of others.	Acknowledge what they have created by their actions and what still remains to be done.	Ask: "What have we created by collaborating?" Ask: "What is still missing for our commitments to be fully realized?" Ask: "What's next?"	Call attention only to the failures and mistakes of others, and ignore or discount the successes of others. Document the actions of self or others when expectations are not being met.	There is acknowledgment of what has been accomplished as a group and as individuals, and of what is still missing. There is interest in moving ahead to create what is missing. The capacity to create collaboratively is growing.

Transition Questions:

- What is now present that we committed to have by this time?
- What is still missing that we committed to have by this time?
- What else is present that contributes to what we want?
- What else is missing that we now want?

rely on people's experience of being acknowledged by teammates as the indicator.

Considering these questions entails making assessments that are based on the results clarified during Commitment, the approach established during Capability, and the actions spelled out during Responsibility.

The first question is "What have we created by collaborating that contributes to reaching our goals and realizing our values?" Not only does this question provide information about progress, it also offers recognition of what the group and individuals have contributed.

The second question is "What is still missing that needs to be in place for our commitments to be fully realized?" Groups may need some practice using this question because speaking this way is not common. When something hasn't been done, rather than looking to what is missing for it to be complete, we tend to blame those we think are responsible and point out how they have fallen short.

Focusing on what is missing rather than what is wrong has a noticeable influence on the climate of the team because blaming tends to divide the team, while identifying what is missing tends to pull the team together to take on the next steps.

The third question is "Given what is missing, where should we put our efforts now so that we will realize our goals and values?" This clarifies and updates priorities for action so that resources are again directed toward the desired results. Once people are comfortable using these questions, they are often shortened to

"What's present?"

"What's missing?"

"What's next?"

Relationship of Acknowledgment to Responsibility and Mutual Understanding

In the flow of the Mobius Model, Acknowledgment leads into Mutual Understanding and is preceded by Responsibility.

Responsibility creates the action plan and also entails carrying out that plan. Since the actions were selected in order to reach certain goals, it is natural to look to assess what progress has been made in achieving them.

Those things that are acknowledged as present can be celebrated, those that are seen as missing can be the object of further collaborative action, and those that are seen differently by different people can be the focus of a conversation for Mutual Understanding. Thus Acknowledgment is the completion of one cycle of creative dialogue and the beginning of another.

Having followed the path of relationship development to its conclusion, it is clear that the end is also the beginning of another adventure *if we choose*. No matter how much we understand each other, there is always more new territory to discover and explore. The Mobius Model can be useful when only one member of a relationship understands it, but it can be even more helpful when all parties are familiar with it. The next chapter illustrates how this map can guide various development adventures, including those involving hundreds of people in dialogue.

CHAPTER FOUR

❧ ❧ ❧ ❧ ❧

Applications of the Mobius Model

Any model that proposes to be a guide for development is only valuable to the extent that it is useful in real applications. If you are a leader of any kind, at any level; if you are a facilitator for development as a consultant, a teacher, a parent, a social worker, or any number of other occupations, you will find that with practice the Mobius Model will provide crucial guidance. It is particularly useful in times of conflict, confusion, or what seem to be insurmountable challenges.

The Mobius Model is a guide for those who facilitate or lead the development of individuals, groups, organizations, and communities. Facilitating development includes coaching individuals, leadership development, team building, strategic planning, and community building. The Mobius Model can be used to design and facilitate effective meetings and agendas, launch new ventures, develop parenting and teaching skills, and build effective and satisfying doctor-patient relationships, to name a few of its uses. The model is also useful as a personal road map for creating effective interactions and relationships with everyone in our lives. We will return to its use as a personal guide after we explore the use of the model for facilitation.

COACHING

Clients usually arrive for coaching with a "negative" monologue about something that is wrong and that points to how they or someone else needs to change. The coaching conversation begins with the transformation of the clients' monologue from what is currently "wrong" (what they *don't want*) in their life or work to a clear vision and commitment to what they *do want*. For the vision to be effective, it must define a possibility that all the stakeholders in the vision will also want. This last point is crucial.

Our coaching clients are often in leadership positions in organizations. One use of the model is to provide a guide to develop more effective leadership skills. For example, a frequent challenge for leaders is to formulate a vision that articulates the common ground for the key stakeholders in such a way that they commit to the vision and work to accomplish it. Great leaders are often those who know how to listen and learn from those they lead. An important role of the coach is to prepare the leader for dialogue with their stakeholders.

Effective leadership is important for any group or organization to succeed, so establishing a coaching relationship with the leader is necessary in any project that intends to support development. Because leadership coaching is often essential for success, the following example provides more detail than the other examples in this chapter.

Coaching is a Creative Dialogue that flows clockwise inside the Mobius Model. Following is an example of the highlights of a coaching conversation with a team leader.

Mutual Understanding

- The client shares his point of view about his current situation.

  "I need to be more assertive. I'm getting overwhelmed by the folks who report to me."

- The coach listens to understand until the client confirms that he feels understood. As the coach listens in this way, the client often shares more deeply.

  "I'm afraid I wasn't cut out to be a leader. I'm afraid my boss was never convinced that I could be successful, either."

- It is important that the coach listens compassionately, but does not agree, disagree, or commiserate with the client's "negative" point of view. If the coach agrees, she will not have an alternative point of view to offer the client, and the coaching may be a waste of time and resources. To facilitate and support development for the client, the coach must trust that a new possibility for the client will emerge from the coaching dialogue. The coach must be a source of possibility in the face of the client's likely conviction that things seem hopeless and he has no idea what to do next. If the coach does not believe that new possibilities—ones that will seem real to the client and the coach—will emerge for the client, then she should decline to coach.

Possibility

- The coach helps the client envision a possibility for himself by asking, "What is now missing that, if it were present, you wouldn't be saying something is wrong?"

  "I wouldn't be afraid of people. I would stop being controlled by others."

- Envisioning a positive possibility is not easy, especially when we feel upset. The coach may need to offer some help, as follows:

  COACH: "If you weren't afraid, what re-

sults would be visible to you and your team that aren't visible now?"

"I would feel confident of my leadership. Upper management would listen to me and value what I say, and I would be advocating effectively for the team. Team members would trust me and talk with me more. They would work with me to establish and accomplish goals."

- The client begins to envision creative possibilities to replace his negative monologues. The coach can add a perspective to discover new ways of understanding the situation.

  COACH: "And your boss would be expressing confidence in your leadership?"

  "Yes!"

- The result is mutual understanding of a new possibility.

Commitment

- The coaching contract is established when coach and client share a commitment to clear and "positive" results. The coach might say something like this:

  COACH: "I think you want

  1. Mutual respect and trust between you and your team members.
  2. Commitment to processes that get results by all team members.
  3. Management support for the team's objectives.
  4. Acknowledgment from your manager that you are an effective leader.

  Am I correct? Is there anything you want to add to this list to be able to say the coaching was a success?"

- The coach and the individual mutually commit to create the results that they have envisioned. The coach proposes a timeline, a process, and a cost for the client to consider for final agreement.

Capability

- When coach and client have agreed to a contract, they look together at ways to create the capability to get the results.

This may include teaching and training on the part of the coach and/or others, or the creation of partnerships that complement the clients' skills and talents.

COACH: "Do you think your manager and your team would want these same results?"

"Yes, sure."

COACH: "Let's look together at ways to invite them to collaborate with you to get these results."

- The coach offers a perspective on how to get the results.

COACH: "I think it will be important to start by listening to the members of your team to hear their concerns. Let's create your vision of success to share with the team. Then you can ask them to share their points of view about what is missing in your vision that they would need to see present before they commit. It is also an opportunity for the team to see that you are interested, are confident, and want to hear and understand them. I propose we explore your vision of success, then design a way to share your vision with the team and practice listening skills. Does that work for you?"

Responsibility

- The client takes responsibility for learning, practicing, and creating the necessary partnerships in the organization. The coach may help facilitate the development of some of the necessary partnerships—in this case, with the team members and upper management. This could be facilitating a dialogue between the client and his team members. It might be facilitating the conversation between the client's manager and the client to agree to measures of success for the client, or other facilitating roles as a partner to the client.

Acknowledgment

- Together, coach and client acknowledge results as they occur, and commit to

new, more challenging results if appropriate.

After some time working with this leader, the client reported:

"It worked! Management is on board for the team's vision, and they have given us the budget to get it done! Now my manager has suggested that I write a report about this project and distribute it throughout the division. I'm feeling a little nervous about that idea."

COACH: "What would you need in order to say, 'I'm ready for the challenge?'"

- New possibilities are envisioned, and potential results identified for commitment, yes or no, to further coaching. If the client chooses additional coaching, another Mobius-guided dialogue will begin. If not, having reached the clear measurable results set out in the original contract, the coaching ends.

In this example, coaching began when the client asked for personal help. It could have begun when he asked for help for his team by saying something like, "Many of my team members are aggressive and don't listen. Could you work with the team to change that?"

TEAM BUILDING

One key benefit of using the Mobius Model as a guide for team building is the facilitation of real commitment before a contract is signed (or a formal project is otherwise initiated). If it is true that satisfying results are only possible when real commitment is present, then it is important to facilitate commitment of key stakeholders to shared results *before* starting to do team building. It's important to facilitate agreement to results when saying no to team building is still a real possibility. The facilitator will need to provide the opportunity for key stakeholders to meet and find common ground about the results they want from any commitment of their time and resources. If the result is a decision to move ahead with team building, or some other form of development activity, the groundwork will be in place for real success.

The process of facilitating commitment to results for team building begins with the identification by the stakeholders of what is present, and what is missing, for them to say they are a successful team (Mutual Understanding). Transformation of what is wrong to what is missing and what is desirable will identify possible results for the team building (Possibility). If the stakeholders say that they are committed to working toward the results identified (Commitment), then the official team building can begin and success is likely.

Team building often begins by establishing a coaching relationship with the leader of the team. For any organization development process to be effective, the leader must be a full partner with the facilitator. Very often, the fact that the leader demonstrates that she can listen in a new way, and understand respectfully even when she doesn't agree, opens up possibilities for the team members that seemed impossible to them before.

When *Mutual Understanding* is present, team members evaluate the vision offered by the leader by saying what works about it and what is missing for them to commit to the vision. The facilitator or the leader will help members translate what they "don't want" into what they "do want." In most cases, the "do wants" are things everyone, including the leader, wants as well, and the items are added to the list of *Possibilities*.

The team prioritizes the list of possibilities to establish team *Commitments* to goals and values. Goals are results they want present at a specific time in the future, e.g., a product ready for market by the end of the fourth quarter. Values are conditions the team wants present at all times, e.g., open, honest communication around team issues.

The whole team, or subgroups of it, develops action plans to create the necessary *Capabilities*. When the action plans are complete, *Responsibilities* can be agreed to, establishing who will do what by when.

Acknowledgment of what is present and what

is still missing for the realization of the shared goals and commitments is crucial for effective and creative interactions to continue. Developing an effective team is an ongoing process that is often initiated by the mutual recognition that something is wrong. If members listen respectfully, in dialogue, they will discover what is missing that they want to create, and the Mobius process will continue.

STRATEGIC PLANNING: A MOBIUS APPROACH

Strategic planning developed in the 1960s as a leadership tool for positioning organizations to maintain their effectiveness in changing environments. Since strategy has traditionally been the province of boards and top managers of organizations, strategic plans were often kept secret from all but a few insiders. The desired outcomes of strategic planning include the formulation of (a) assumptions about the external and internal conditions that need to be taken into account in positioning the organization, (b) clarity about mission and values, and (c) priorities among strategic objectives for guiding action.

By 1994, the value of strategic planning was being called into question. In *The Rise and Fall of Strategic Planning,* Henry Mintzberg pointed to three potentially fatal flaws of strategic planning as it was being practiced:

- Discontinuities undermine assumptions that the future will be like the past.
- Planners are too often detached from the realities of the organization.
- Strategy emerges from a chaotic, synthesizing process, not a linear, analytic process.

Two additional challenges should be added:

- Any plan is limited by the viewpoints of those who participate in its development.
- All plans fail if those responsible for implementation do not understand or want

the results, or do not like the means required to deliver the results.

The Mobius Model offers a way of understanding and facilitating strategic planning that overcomes many of these limitations. It provides

- A way to **understand strategic planning** as a clear formulation of the ongoing stakeholder conversations.
- A way to **lead multi-stakeholder dialogues** so that written plans reflect the common ground among the emergent, shared visions, values, and strategic priorities of the stakeholders. The result is committed action and collaboration among all the stakeholders.

While no plan can anticipate all discontinuities in change, the planning process can create the conditions that keep an organization's strategic vision responsive to emergent challenges.

From the perspective provided by the Mobius Model, strategic planning is a facilitated dialogue that expands to include a microcosm of stakeholder viewpoints. It results in

- Mutual Understanding of the current situation.
- Shared vision of emergent Possibilities.
- Commitment to priorities among goals, values, and timelines to guide collaborative action.
- Tactical planning (Capability) results in agreement on effective actions.
- Agreement to Responsibilities for action ensures accountability.
- Responsiveness to change: strategic planning requires agreement to ongoing evaluation of results and periodic re-evaluation (Acknowledgment) of the mission, vision, values, and goals.

It is important that strategic planning be an ongoing planning process. Skilled champions of key initiatives are essential to lead the implementation of the priority goals and values. Champions maintain momentum by regular acknowledgment of successes and revision of the plan as necessary.

The following case study illustrates some key Mobius Model principles, which are articulated in the subsequent section.

A Case Study

Key stakeholders in a large, suburban public works department were guided by the Mobius Model in developing the first department-wide strategic plan, in partnership with Mobius, Inc. consultants. While the process may differ in some details from strategic planning within other organizations, it illustrates using stakeholder dialogue as a general approach to strategic planning.

- The director of the public works department was dedicated and thoughtful about the strategic priorities for his departments, but he had not clearly communicated his thinking to others. Dialogues for Mutual Understanding and Possibility with the consulting team enabled the director to articulate clear, realistic departmental goals, values, and three-year and one-year priorities. He practiced *listening for understanding* with us and then brought his proposed goals and values to his management team to evaluate. He *listened to understand* what was present and what was missing for them to commit to these goals and values. It was very important to the team that he listened fully, without argument. We facilitated the conversation so that when one of the managers said that something was wrong with the director's vision, we invited that person to say what he would need to see something he perceived as missing in the present, as possible in the future instead. This transformed what was "wrong" into a possibility. For example, the statement,

"This list of values doesn't say anything about what the work environment should be like. We don't value our employees!" is a *what's wrong* statement. *What would you like to see?* is a transforming question. "I want a value that says, 'To respect, encourage, and support employees'" is a statement of what is now missing that may be possible to create in the future.

- In dialogue with the managers, additions were incorporated into a draft strategic plan (Possibility) and taken to the supervisors in focus groups for evaluation and input. The consulting team worked with the supervisors to translate what they said did not work into statements about what they wanted. Again, the key here is to facilitate the transformation of what is not wanted (what's wrong) into what is wanted that would be fully satisfying. There is usually disagreement about what is wrong and whose fault it is, but very little disagreement about positive results for the future.

- The supervisors' additions were brought back to the management team and incorporated into the draft of the plan in red ink so that it was clear to all what was added by the supervisors.

- This draft of the plan went in a timely way to focus groups of all the employees. Again, whatever in the draft plan "didn't work" for them was transformed into possibilities, and then communicated to the management team and incorporated into the plan, this time in blue ink.

- The city manager made additions to the plan in gold ink.

- The whole department of sixty people came together for a dialogue about the plans with all the additions visible in the different colored inks. The management team began by sharing with all of the employees what they had heard the employees saying in their additions to the plan. Then each department head (management team member) sat in a circle of about ten employees who did not report to him or her to encourage open communication. They listened respectfully to what the employees wanted so that the employees knew they were understood. There was a great sense of respect for the employee point of view demonstrated in this process. At the end of the meeting, all the participants were asked if they could support the strategic goals and values articulated in the plan. All said yes and, while some were skeptical about management's commitment to follow through, everyone said that it had been a positive and fruitful meeting, and they had real hope that the department could move ahead effectively with the plan.

- Finally, other stakeholders—the other citywide department heads, the city council members, and representative citizens—were given an opportunity to evaluate the plan and share their point of view with the director. In future cycles of strategic planning, these outside stakeholders will participate more fully in the planning process.

This case study illustrates the use of principles embodied in the Mobius Model to guide a strategic planning process. It provides a way for key stakeholders to challenge the assumptions of leaders responsible for formulating organizational strategy. Leaders shared their points of view and then listened respectfully to learn what worked and what was missing for other stakeholders to commit. They expanded their understanding and incorporated new viewpoints as the dialogue expanded. When ideas were not incorporated, the rationale for the decision was communicated so the stakeholders were able to recognize that their point of view had been fully understood and taken into account. When timelines and priorities were established, Commitment for action emerged for all of the employees and the other key stakeholders. Since this was the first strategic planning process for the organization, healthy skepticism remained about the likelihood of follow-through on commitments, but the commitments and accountabilities were clear.

Some Key Mobius Principles

The first Mobius principle is that the greater the diversity of stakeholder viewpoints, the more grounded the vision of the whole that emerges. By engaging widely differing stakeholder viewpoints in the dialogue, trust and respect of differing viewpoints increases along with the likelihood of ongoing dialogue after the plan is written. Participants become aware of the impact of change on other stakeholders as they develop new ways to communicate with each other. In this way, the shared vision, mutually recognized in the planning process, can continue to evolve in response to change. By scheduling a strategic planning cycle, regular periods dedicated to reflection and dialogue about the state of the organization, it is possible to recognize and adapt strategy to emergent issues.

A second principle is that the common ground (shared vision) among diverse perspectives can be recognized and expanded only as differences are mutually understood and incorporated. The dialogue process embodied in the Mobius Model provides a way to transform conflict and problem-focused conversations in an organization into a source of information about the whole system. By including all stakeholder perspectives in the strategic dialogue, organizational leaders invite others to challenge their assumptions and increase the likelihood that the vision and priorities that emerge are grounded in a shared understanding of current reality.

A third Mobius principle is that committed action follows from Mutual Understanding and shared Possibilities. Because the strategic dialogue includes a microcosm of stakeholder viewpoints, including those responsible for implementing strategic priorities, the likelihood of stakeholder commitment is greatly increased. Commitment is missing when stakeholders do not feel they have a

voice, or when they do not believe the strategy is realistic. While plans can be implemented by compliant, uncommitted stakeholders, the result is a loss of effectiveness, satisfaction, and creativity. Each time leaders expand the dialogue to include more diverse viewpoints, the vision, values, goals, and priorities become more robust and increase the likelihood of committed action and collaboration.

From a Mobius perspective, strategic planning is a creative dialogue that includes many layers of stakeholders in Mutual Understanding, visioning Possibilities and Commitment to goals and values. When the strategic plan is complete, tactical plans are developed (Capability) and Responsibilities are determined. Strategic planning includes ongoing processes for evaluation, timelines for completion, and periodic reevaluation (Acknowledgment) of the strategic goals and values. It is important that processes for ongoing planning be incorporated in the plan and that skilled champions lead the initiatives for priority goals and values. In this way, momentum is maintained by regular acknowledgment of successes and revision of the plan as necessary.

The responsibility of leaders in strategic planning is to recognize when to initiate the strategic dialogue, plan how it will be facilitated, participate fully by sharing their vision, *listen to understand,* and communicate their strategic choices in ways that respect differing stakeholder viewpoints. In this way, the strategic dialogue maintains a creative vitality that leads to committed action.

COMMUNITY BUILDING

Usually, when developing community relationships, you are not dealing with one overarching organization. This means that effective communication with key stakeholders may be very difficult. Enrolling impassioned individuals representing the different stakeholder points of view is the key to success.

A very large school district, for example, was informed that federal funding for special education was to be severely cut. The front page of the metropolitan newspaper ran many stories about the passionate feelings on every side of the issue, especially those around funding for children defined as emotionally and behaviorally disordered (EBD). A vocal and angry group of parents, with children in regular education classes, did not want to see any resources moved from their children to the EBD children. Teachers, administrators, parents, social workers, police officers, and politicians lined up on both sides of the issue, creating bad feelings throughout the community. The director of special education had the foresight to look for a process to facilitate mutual understanding and generate new possibilities.

Mutual Understanding, Possibility, and Commitment

- A "design team" of seventy people representing each passionately held point of view met for two days to agree to a definition of success for a communitywide dialogue. They sat in mixed circles, full of apprehension, and were asked to listen to understand. The turning point in the event came when everyone gathered to observe a dialogue between the special education director and the leader of the angry, "regular ed" parents. It was a tense and highly charged moment, but they observed the discovery of common ground between the two and, as a result, committed to work to bring members of their constituency together for three days of dialogue with the hope that they would experience similar results.

- Out of their commitment, the initial seventy people enlisted enough others so that 180 people, representing equal numbers of each stakeholder group, came together for three full days of dialogue. Evidence of success came into view at this event when the different stakeholder groups (special education teachers, regular teachers, social workers, parents on both sides) declared that they did not want to be placed in groups with those with whom they shared a point of view. They wanted instead to continue to sit in mixed groups, where common ground was emerging and new possibilities created hope. At the end of the three days, participants in the dialogue were quoted in the newspaper as saying that they had not dared to hope that the dialogue would make a difference, but that indeed they felt real optimism about the future for all children in the district.

- Politicians arrived for the last half-day of dialogue and heard reports from the participants about the possibilities that had emerged and requests for their support.

Capability, Responsibility, and Acknowledgment

- Seventy of the 180 people agreed to gather for collaborative action planning to support the education and well-being of all children in the community. Action plans for each of the outcomes from the three-day dialogue were presented and approved by the group as a whole. The participants said that one of the key outcomes of their time together was the creation of real respect and understanding among those who work to serve the needs of children. These new relationships enabled teachers, social workers, police officers, and others to collaborate in their services and create a much more unified and supportive system for children.

- The participants agreed to a process and time line for revisiting the plans and the success of the collaboration. One year later, key stakeholders confirmed that the ongoing collaboration was making a real difference in their ability to serve the needs of the children in the district.

FACILITATING RELATIONSHIP DEVELOPMENT

The process of facilitating relationship development is essentially the same for groups of any size—a Creative Dialogue that includes all stakeholders in an expanding Mobius conversation. Communitywide dialogues of 2,000 folks, representing an even larger stakeholder base, can be successfully facilitated to result in shared commitments to goals and values, and action plans to accomplish the goals.

When using the Mobius Model as a guide to facilitate relationship development, it is important to listen carefully to the conversations in the group to discover where monologues are blocking effective interactions. For example, when the conversation is about being confused, it means that commitments are not clear. In the Mobius Model, Possibility precedes Commitment, so you will need to find out if possibilities are clear and feel realistic to the participants. If shared possibilities are not in view (e.g., the boss says it's possible, but no one else buys it), the conversation needs to go back to create Mutual Understanding of the differing points of view. When no one is taking responsibility, find out if there is commitment to action plans to develop the necessary skills and resources (Capability). (See chapter 3 for descriptions of what it is like when any of the qualities is missing.)

Mobius facilitators contract with clients only after all the key stakeholders commit to work toward achieving agreed-upon results. This can involve quite a bit of work up front to facilitate the commitment of the key stakeholders, but we have found that success is possible only when all parties are committed to results that they agree are worth their time and money to work toward.

THE MOBIUS MODEL AS A PERSONAL GUIDE FOR SUCCESSFUL RELATIONSHIPS

Whenever you notice that you or someone else holds the point of view that something or someone is wrong, there is an opportunity to use the Mobius Model as a personal road map for Creative Dialogue. This is especially challenging if the stories from others about what is wrong are about you. However, if you can listen to understand compassionately, you can begin a dialogue that will make a great contribution to your relationship. When you feel misunderstood, it is usually true that the other person feels misunderstood as well. Because you have noticed that you feel misunderstood, you are in a place to choose to be the first listener. If you listen well, trust will be created and the speaker will go deeper into his point of view, allowing you greater understanding of his thoughts and feelings. When he feels fully understood, he will probably be interested in hearing your perspective. When Mutual Understanding is present, the dialogue will flow to Possibility and so on, as long as listening for understanding is present as each element of the dialogue unfolds.

It is also possible for development to happen even if one person in the relationship is not willing to listen for Mutual Understanding. If I listen when the other person will not, then I am able to expand my own view and see and understand in ways that I cannot see alone. This expanded understanding often leads to compassion, and from compassion can flow well-being in the relationship. Those who can listen in this way are expressing a high level of personal development.

Conclusion

❧ ❧ ❧ ❧ ❧

"Tasting the orange" is a metaphor we often use for the experience of relationship development by choice. It's very difficult to explain what an orange tastes like to someone who has never tasted one. You may have "tasted the orange" before reading *The Mobius Model: A Guide for Developing Effective Relationships, in Groups, Teams, and Organizations.* If not before, we hope that you have now.

We believe that once you have had the experience of choosing to relate creatively when you were upset with another and tempted to try to control or avoid the situation, you will want to do it again and again. Suppose you become aware of one of your familiar blame monologues as someone "stubbornly" opposes what seems to you an obviously good idea. You recognize your temptation to react in the same old way, but choose to engage the other person in dialogue instead. If you get results you like, the chances are good that the other person will like the results as well. The choice for development is available to us anytime we recognize a difference with another individual or group.

In summary, the key assumptions and principles underlying the Mobius Model—a guide for following the path of development—are these:

- The development of human relationships is a natural process that can also be facilitated.
- Monologues mark differences that can either limit development or be a rich resource for increasing the effectiveness and satisfaction of all relationships.
- Dialogue is a unique form of conversation that can transform monologues into resources for the development of the relationships that result in healthy individuals, groups, organizations, and communities.
- The Mobius Model provides an effective road map for conversations that get the results desired by everyone who has a stake in them.
- The Mobius Model can be used as a guide for development of any and all relationships, personal and professional.

Some of the challenges to development present in professional relationships have not been addressed:

- The value of relationship development is not yet compelling to many leaders in organizations. Decision makers often view development as a "touchy-feely" luxury to provide when times are good, but not essential to sustaining productive and healthy organizations. Though the evidence seems overwhelming that the current global situation—accelerating change and increasing interaction of diverse populations—requires an ever-increasing capacity for creative relationships in groups, organizations, communities, and nations, the commitment of many leaders is still missing.

- We have not explained the theory and research basis for the Mobius Model and associated practices (see appendix C, "The Mobius Model as an Integral Theory and Practice"), nor have we explored the relationship of the Mobius Model with other models (see appendix B, "Using the Mobius Model with the Myers-Briggs Type Indicator").

- Only the most basic tools, listening and speaking for mutual understanding, have been described in any detail (see appendix A, "The Mobius Model Instrument for Group Self-Assessment,"

for a description of a much more sophisticated tool for assessing group development).

We hope you will initiate Creative Dialogues within your own network of relationships. As this alternative to conflict and suffering becomes the choice of more and more individuals, the natural process of relationship development will acquire momentum.

Nothing would delight us more than to connect with others who recognize the possibility and importance of developing healthy human relationships. If you are interested in learning more about using the Mobius Model as a guide for development, using the Mobius Model Instrument (MMI), or becoming a trained Mobius facilitator, please visit our Web site: www.mobiusmodel.com.

Appendices

❧ ❧ ❧ ❧ ❧

APPENDIX A

The Mobius Model Instrument
for Group Self-Assessment

APPENDIX B

Using the Mobius Model with the
Myers-Briggs Type Indicator

APPENDIX C

The Mobius Model as an
Integral Theory and Practice

The Mobius Model Instrument for Group Self-Assessment

As a leader of groups or a facilitator of group development, you understand why hard-working members usually say their plates are too full. If they can't find enough time to get their work done, how can they take time to work on being a more effective team? On the other hand, they know they should. You also know that any group, no matter how good, can be more effective if they just make the changes that everyone already knows will make a difference. You don't want to waste their time on tests and exercises that they won't find useful or that won't result in action, but you know even a little time for reflection could make a difference.

The Mobius Model Instrument (MMI), developed for use by busy teams, can be completed in less than twenty minutes. The MMI Report provides information credible to the group members—their own judgments about what *they* think is important for their success and how often *they* already do those things. How their point of view compares to the group viewpoint appeals to their natural curiosity. In addition, the Mobius Model provides a fresh point of view, allowing them to see their team in a new light: "I've never thought about our group in this way before—this is helpful!"

Every team that has used the MMI has taken immediate action that makes an obvious difference in their effectiveness. Because the charts and graphs allow them to see where they *already* agree about their strengths as a group, as well as their areas of dissatisfaction, they see what they can do that will make the most difference. They do not see the MMI results as the judgment of an outside expert who doesn't understand their situation. Once members of a group complete the MMI, they are eager to know the results, and their conversations lead to committed action.

DESCRIPTION OF THE MOBIUS MODEL INSTRUMENT

The Mobius Model Instrument directly relates to the Mobius Model, and the qualities that are assessed are the six qualities of relationship defined in the Mobius Model: Mutual Understanding, Possibility, Commitment, Capability, Responsibility, and Acknowledgment. Each individual item in the instrument is formulated to reflect one of these qualities. There are six questions for each Mobius quality, and therefore thirty-six questions in the instrument.

As people complete the MMI, they make two ratings for each item. On a four-point scale to the left of each item, respondents make a rating of *frequency* ("For this group, how often is it true that_____?") and *importance* ("For the success of this group, how important is it that_____?"). A Group and Individual Report is generated from the completed instruments. The report compares the frequency and importance ratings both for the whole group and for each individual. The report also indicates the areas of greatest satisfaction, least satisfaction, and variability of viewpoint.

Mobius Model Instrument

For this team, *how often* is it true that
_____?

For the success of this team, *how important* is it
that _____?

Almost never   Critically important
  Sometimes   Important
    Usually   Somewhat important
      Nearly always   Unimportant

O O O O   1. We understand our differing strength and limitations   O O O O

USING THE MOBIUS MODEL
INSTRUMENT WITH GROUPS

The MMI is intended for use by groups who work together and wish to develop or improve their capacity to get results and maintain satisfying relationships. It is used most effectively when the following conditions are present for a group or team:

- Leadership within the organization is committed to supporting and providing resources for individual and group development.
- Group membership is consistent.
- The group or team has agreed to look at and evaluate aspects of their own functioning.
- Members possess communication skills of self-expression, feedback, and listening, or can access resources to improve these skills.
- There is adequate time to discuss and understand the results and decide how to use them.

The MMI is to be used by trained facilitators, who (1) have an understanding of the Mobius Model and its relevance to group development, (2) know how to administer and interpret the instrument, and (3) are able to facilitate a conversation about the results. Training sessions to prepare professionals to use the instrument are provided by the MMI Group, LLC on a regular basis. Completion of the two-day initial training is required to purchase and use the MMI, with a recommendation that persons also attend workshops and seek out other opportunities to extend their understanding of the Mobius Model.

USING THE MOBIUS MODEL
INSTRUMENT FOR TEAM DEVELOPMENT

Based on responses of group members on the MMI, score summaries and a written report (the Group and Individual Report) are generated. The Group and Individual Report is designed to guide the facilitated team dialogues about the results. Each member is provided a copy of the written report, which first presents group results, followed by a section that details the individual's results.

The group results are considered and discussed by the whole group. Members are then given time to privately look at their own results in light of the group dialogue. Each person has an opportunity to share what he or she chooses from his or her own results before the group decides on priorities for development.

Results of the MMI are used by trained facilitators to guide and stimulate dialogues for Mutual Understanding, Possibility, and Commitment. After completion of the dialogue for Mutual Understanding, which results in a shared appreciation of how members view and experience the team, the dialogues for Possibility and Commitment help the group to identify areas for group development and to set priorities, with a commitment of yes or no to take further steps.

A Case Example:
A Mental Health Therapy Team

One of the first work groups to take the MMI was a mental health therapy practice providing counseling services to a diverse, inner-city clientele. The group included two owner-therapists and eight other individuals associated with the practice as independent contractors. Several individuals on the team had collaborated in this way for six to eight years, while two or three others were new to the group. Challenges facing this team included little time to be in dialogue with one another or to work collaboratively, and the financial reality that only time spent face-to-face with clients was "billable time."

The group met once a month for a two-hour staff meeting to review a broad range of personal, professional, and business issues. In December, the owners wanted to find a way to create a shared vision for the coming year that everyone would re-

ally commit to working toward. The group was invited to take the MMI to aid in this endeavor.

The group's composite ratings of the six Mobius qualities, taken from their Group and Individual Report, are in the table below. Some interesting patterns were revealed when the individual viewpoints were summarized together. The qualities that were most highly valued (rated as most important to the success of the group) were Mutual Understanding and Responsibility, consistent with the therapeutic orientation of the group and the need to function independently without much team support or supervision.

For all of the qualities, there was a sizable gap between ratings of importance and ratings of frequency, an indication that this was a group with high ideals and a sense of falling short in meeting those ideals in action. The largest gap, indicating the greatest dissatisfaction, occurred between the ratings of importance and frequency in the Commitment area, suggesting a lack of agreement to *shared* goals and values.

In general, results of the MMI gave concrete data to this team about qualities of relationship that were highly valued by all, and areas to emphasize to make actions more consistent with their

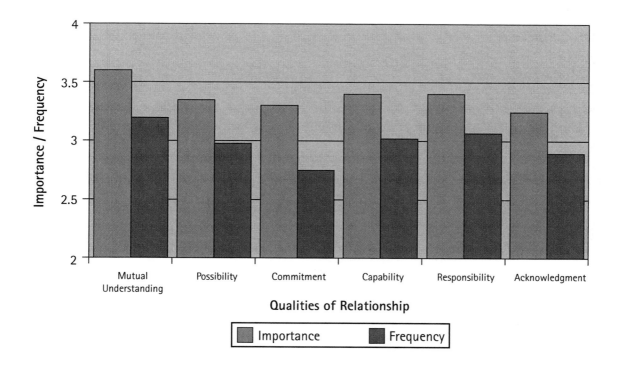

strongly held values. Out of the dialogue to review these results, several action steps were scheduled, including an all-day retreat to clarify a vision and action plan for the coming year. Many individuals commented that the instrument provided a vehicle for members to talk together about issues that had not been discussed previously.

Data from the MMI also helped to highlight the real-world impediments to functioning collaboratively. These included lack of time, the financial disincentive, and the absence of a process of accountability for shared commitments. The group was able to make clear choices about priorities for development that included a grounded sense of the changes that would be needed to be successful.

The Mobius Model Instrument helps to bring about the development of satisfying and effective relationships by stimulating team members to look at the functioning of their group and select the ways in which they would like to grow. The Mobius Model dialogue forms the basis for the team's interactions as they work through the process of exploring their differing views of the team (as reflected in the MMI data), identifying new results they desire, committing to goals and values that support getting those results, and making and carrying out a plan to achieve them.

* * * * *

Using the Mobius Model with the Myers-Briggs Type Indicator®

The Mobius Model can be used in conjunction with other approaches to understanding individuals, groups, and organizations. There is a particularly fruitful fit between the widely used Myers-Briggs Type Indicator (MBTI) and the Mobius Model because of their parallel emphases. The MBTI focuses on the qualities of individuals and their development, while the Mobius Model does the same for relationships. When used together, it becomes clear how each MBTI type brings a unique way of understanding relationships that includes both potential contributions and potential blind spots.

For example, Mutual Understanding values the contribution of each person's point of view and so draws particularly on the feeling function of the MBTI. Those individuals with a preference for feeling typically value this quality and want to take the time needed to listen fully to all—an important contribution to any relationship. However, they may also overemphasize this quality and give insufficient attention to some others that are equally important.

Conversely, those with a preference for thinking may not place enough value on developing Mutual Understanding and consequently move ahead before all parties are fully heard and understood. A similar dynamic can occur with teams. For example, Responsibility exists when there are clear expectations about who will do what by when so that plans can be implemented. This quality draws particularly on the sensing function. Individuals who prefer sensing, as well as many teams and organizations, highly prize taking action. If, however, they move to action too quickly, skipping or underemphasizing other necessary steps, they may later discover that their actions are aimed at a goal that all members don't endorse (i.e., that Commitment is missing) or don't believe is feasible (i.e., that Possibility is missing).

The development of fully satisfying and productive relationships for individuals and teams requires that those involved be able to recognize and use their differences in complementary ways. Combining the MBTI with the Mobius Model provides a way to be aware of which qualities may be over- or undervalued and to direct sufficient attention to all the essential elements.

In conjunction with the Center for Applications of Psychological Type (CAPT) in Gainesville, Florida, the MMI Group offers a workshop on Integrating Psychological Type and the Mobius Model.

Appendix C

❧ ❧ ❧ ❧ ❧

The Mobius Model as an Integral Theory and Practice

This brief section presents a broad overview of theory and practice related to the Mobius Model.

The Mobius Model draws on theory and research from developmental psychology but is not limited by that discipline's focus on development as an individual phenomenon. The wide-ranging work of Ken Wilber, a twenty-first century philosopher, is a great resource for anyone interested in the ways in which the idea of development has emerged in many cultural traditions. Wilber uses the systems concept of the holon to expand developmental theory beyond the individual:

> A holon is a whole that is part of other wholes. For example, a whole atom is part of a whole molecule, a whole molecule is part of a whole cell, a whole cell is part of a whole organism, and so on. . . . The universe is fundamentally composed of holons, wholes that are parts of other wholes. Letters are parts of words which are parts of sentences which are parts of entire languages. A person is part of a family which is part of a community which is part of a nation which is part of the globe, and so on. (Ken Wilber, "Integral Psychology," *The Collected Works of Ken Wilber, Volume Four* [Boston: Shambhala Publications, Inc., 1999], 439)

Wilber has developed an integral theory that delineates the different ways humans, at every level of holon—individual, partner, group, organization, community, and beyond—function at each stage of development. While a full exploration of these far-ranging phenomena is not possible in this brief account, one fascinating implication suggested by Wilber is worth noting. The many stages of human development delineated in various theories can be condensed to three: pre-rational, rational, and post-rational stages. Western science and technology, which emerged during the Enlightenment period, has been an impetus to the development of rational ways of thinking and acting in the West. However, most scientists and observers of science agree that science has its limits as a way of understanding, especially in understanding and judging matters of value—goodness and beauty, for example. Wilber believes that available research suggests that, from a developmental perspective, our dominant culture is based in a rational worldview, though most of us function much of the time in pre-rational ways, and some of us, some of the time, function in post-rational ways.

Wilber calls for the development of integral practices that facilitate the natural process of human development consistent with integral theory. Don Beck has drawn on Wilber's work in an attempt to put developmental theory into a practice for changing whole socio-cultural systems, including the transformation of apartheid in South Africa. His model, Spiral Dynamics, describes worldviews—i.e., ways of understanding and interacting that are associated with each stage of human development. In healthy humans, each stage of development incorporates the preceding stage and develops new, more complex, and more effective ways of understanding and interacting. He has designated each developmental level by a color and formulated the key elements of the worldview associated with the color/level. By helping participants in a system to understand and appreciate the different ways in which they, and others, understand and interact in their system, new ways (Possibilities) come into view, and the grip of the old ways loosens. The qualities of relationship identified in the Mobius Model and the worldviews associated with each stage of development in Spiral Dynamics can be mapped as follows: Rational self-interest is indicated by orange in Beck's model, which corresponds to Capability. It is preceded by the irrational, mythic (blue) stage, Responsibility, and followed by a post-rational (green) stage, Commitment, and so on. Wilber says research indicates that, as a species, we are at a point in our development where the rational worldview, exemplified by corporations and our current political system, is developing toward a post-rational (green) worldview. However, the emerging (green) worldview is not well developed and remains unstable.

Wilber points out that there are *individuals*, in every tradition, who develop post-rational levels of understanding and ways of interacting. Those able to access these levels remain fully rational but are able to recognize larger, coherent patterns of life that are not discernable by logic and data alone. However influential these post-rational individuals have become as teachers and exemplars, most human beings are not yet able to sustain even rational ways of understanding and interacting with each other when their worldviews conflict.

We see the Mobius Model as a contribution to the development of an integral theory and practice as outlined by Ken Wilber. Individuals, partners, groups, organizations, and larger human systems can be guided by the Mobius Model to use their differences, at any level of holon or stage of development, to move together beyond differing, self-interested viewpoints to recognize common ground and possibilities that cannot be accessed by individuals reasoning alone. Once recognized, a shared, post-rational vision makes rational sense to those with differing viewpoints. This shared vision can become the common ground for shared commitments and action.

The Mobius Model provides a guide to post-rational ways of understanding and interacting, through dialogue, that respects reason but points beyond the limits of reason. This is a far different and more mutually satisfying strategy than the regression to pre-rational feelings grounded in ethnocentric or group-based viewpoints that acknowledge no value, only error, in the viewpoints of those who differ. It is not necessary to adopt a developmental theory to enjoy the fruits of dialogue, but developmental theory can provide a way to acknowledge all that reason and technology bring to human life while recognizing the need for still "deeper" levels of understanding. The Mobius Model assumes that our individual and collective well-being results from actions based in a recognition of the coherence among parts and wholes at *all* levels.

The MMI Group, LLC

❧ ❧ ❧ ❧ ❧

Larry Demarest, Ph.D., is a trainer, writer, and organizational consultant. He uses the MBTI instrument in organizations, presents type workshops nationally and internationally, and is the author of *Looking at Type in the Workplace* and *Out of Time: How the 16 Types Manage Time and Work*. He's a bird-watcher and delights in an annual canoe trip in northern Minnesota.

Marjorie Herdes, co-president of Mobius, Inc. Organization Development Consultants since 1991, worked as a quality improvement specialist at Honeywell, Inc. before becoming a consultant. Her educational background is politics, Arab studies, and education. She has been a teacher-trainer and consultant to schools in the United States and Brazil, and a political analyst for the Department of the Army. She is game for any kind of outdoor adventure.

Joyce Stockton, Ph.D., Licensed Psychologist, Licensed School Psychologist, is co-director of the Well-Family Clinic in St. Paul, Minnesota, where she has been working with children of all ages and their families for over twenty-five years. An experienced therapist, diagnostician, and systems consultant, she also provides individual counseling for adults and couples and family therapy. Joyce delights in travel, sailing, and camping with her kids and grandkids.

Will Stockton, Ph.D., co-president of Mobius Inc., cultural anthropologist, and the originator of the Mobius Model, has facilitated collaboration and development in multinational companies, nonprofit organizations, and the public sector for over twenty-five years. He taught for ten years at the University of Minnesota, conducted field research on culture conflict, and has published and taught in the areas of human development, education, and health care. He provides leadership in the implementation of the Mobius Model in the work of the Well-Family Clinic. Will is the skipper on sailing adventures with family and friends on Lake Superior and in the Caribbean.